MICHIGAN RIVERS LESS PADDLED:

THE RIVERS, THE TOWNS, THE TAVERNS

Michigan Rivers Less Paddled: The Rivers, The Towns, The Taverns
© Doc Fletcher, 2009

ISBN - 978-1-933926-19-3

Arbutus Press
Traverse City, Michigan
editor@arbutuspress.com
www.Arbutuspress.com

First Edition/ First Printing

Printed and bound in the United States of America

Data source for maps: 2006 ESRI Data and Maps and Michigan Center for Geographic Information.

Maps © Arbutus Press, 2009
Photos © Doc Fletcher, 2009

Illustrations Bigtimeartguy Inc. - Keith Jones, 2009

MICHIGAN RIVERS LESS PADDLED:

THE RIVERS, THE TOWNS, THE TAVERNS

DOC FLETCHER

ARBUTUS PRESS ~TRAVERSE CITY, MICHIGAN

CONTENTS

DEDICATION

To our mothers, shining stars Mary & Ruthe

"WHEREVER THERE IS A CHANNEL FOR WATER,
THERE IS A ROAD FOR THE CANOE."

HENRY DAVID THOREAU

PREFACE

Michigan Rivers Less Paddled: The Rivers, The Towns, The Taverns is the title of this book, but in many ways it could be considered Volume II of my first book, *Weekend Canoeing in Michigan*. There is a great deal of continuity between the two books:

1)   Only rivers serviced by a canoe or kayak livery are included, so that this book can be a guide for folks who love to get out there on the rivers, but may not own their own boats.

2)   For each river, a suggested trip is outlined with information including that river's degree of difficulty i.e. Is it family friendly? Does it have fast water? Local livery details and miles to the livery from various towns in Michigan and from Milwaukee (in honor of the birthplace of Pabst Blue Ribbon). Included are key landmarks and obstacles you will encounter on the water, and time needed to complete each trip.

3)   Interesting historical stories about a nearby town, and where to find the local Detroit Tiger radio affiliate on the radio dial.

4)   You are directed to a local old time tavern, one that your grandfather would be comfortable in, so you can relax and relive the day on the river over a burger and a cold one.

5)   From each river trip, a quote of the day plus a sound track inspired by that river.

No matter where you are in Michigan, you'll be within a 2 hour drive of at least one of the rivers and canoe liveries in this book. Included are both Upper and Lower Peninsula rivers, as well as a mix of meandering and fast flowing waterways.

The "Kenny sez" words of wisdom & fun comments were inspired by conversations while floating down the rivers with my crack research team companions. The crack researcher that accompanied me on more rivers than anyone else was Kenny Umphrey, also known as Kanoo Kenny. Each and every one of the crack researchers was helpful in the creation of this book, and I've noted their presence in each river chapter.

Whether you're out on the water with family, a church group, or just a few friends, here are a few river tips for your consideration:

1)   Rule #1: respect others on the river. Show appreciation for the wonderful experience of floating down a beautiful river. If you're in a big group, tone it down when floating near others, especially families. Watch your language. There's nothing that's cooler than doing the right thing on the river.

2)   Don't leave wet river shoes in your vehicle overnight, or you'll experience a smell you'll not soon forget. Maggie says, "Or your car will stink to high heaven."

3)   If the livery owner tells you that the river warrants wearing a life vest, do it.

4)   Don't leave trash on the river or at the campgrounds.

5)   The river abounds with visual delights – don't forget your camera. The photos that I've taken for this book were with my waterproof Olympus digital camera.

6)   "Chow Time is Important" (thanks Wayne!). You don't want your growling stomach to drown out the wildlife.

Within "The Town" segment of several chapters are references to the Potawatomi Indian tribe. Across a spectrum of very respected sources, the tribe's name is spelled in a variety of ways including Pottawatomie, Potawatomie, and Pottowattomie. For simplicity and consistency sake, the Potawatomi spelling is used in all chapters.

At the back of the book is a list of Michigan canoe and kayak liveries, and a paddling and camping checklist, in an effort to assist you with your river trip planning process.

Happy Paddling!
Doc Fletcher

INTRODUCTION

This book was born of a desire to explore those Michigan rivers that are less traveled, rivers that don't quickly or ever come to mind when one thinks of the state's waterways. This book allows me to actively promote two of my loves: canoeing and Michigan. But most of all, this book gives me an excuse to keep on paddling.

ACKNOWLEDGEMENTS

To Maggie, my wife and best friend, for her love, hugs, and smiles. For her genuine enthusiasm, support, and participation in my research and writing. ~~ To my Mom & Dad, who never shorted their children on love and attention.
 ~~ To the retailers and dotcoms that carry my books, my family and friends who work to sell the books, and the readers who buy them.
~~ To Arbutus Press: Susan for believing enough to publish me, and to Susan and Gail for their promotional assistance.

To my crack researchers who tirelessly find ways to get out with me on the rivers, in the towns, and at the taverns, and come up with the details and facts that might otherwise be overlooked.

To my 4Day brother Jonesy, aka Keith Jones, for the artist wizardry of his alter ego, Big Time Art Guy. Thanks for the wonderful illustrations.

To all of the chamber of commerce employees, librarians, local historians, fellow canoers met on the rivers, and tavern-folk who share knowledge about their rivers, their towns, and their taverns.

To Stephanie Webb, Catherine Behrendt, & Eddie Rucker *WZZM's "Take Five"*, Jayne Bower *WWJ*, Shelley Irwin *WGVU*, Pam Fleming *Northville Record/Novi News*, Gerry Barnaby *WLHT* , Dianna Stampfler *Promote Michigan*, Ellen Creager *Detroit Free Press*, Lori Rackl *Chicago Sun Times*, Sandi Weindling *Lake Magazine* , Jerry Nunn *Bay City Times*, Charlie Mahler *Canoeing.com*, Linda Twardowski *Traverse the Magazine www.mynorth.com*, Mike Ingels *The Erie Hiker,* Kurt Kuban *Canton Observer & Eccentric* for the reviews and interviews and for getting the word out.

To all the canoers and kayakers who come to the book signings and to the State Park & Library book talks. Your passion and feedback make it fun. To my Guardian Angels for working around the clock on my behalf. Thank God for my abundant blessings in family and in friends (my spiritual sisters and brothers), and for allowing me to understand that true happiness lies in doing the right thing and in having gratitude for what blessings we have.

Thank God for my abundant blessings in family and in friends (my spiritual sisters and brothers), and for allowing me to understand that true happiness lies in doing the right thing and in having gratitude for what blessings we have.

RIVERS LESS PADDLED IN MICHIGAN'S UPPER PENINSULA

THE AU TRAIN RIVER AU TRAIN, MICHIGAN

RIVER SOUNDTRACK:
Black Widow – Alice Cooper & Vincent Price
Give Me Central 209 – Lighting Hopkins
The Ballad of Jed Clampett – Flatt & Scruggs
Spooky – Classics IV
Comin' Home – The Third Power

RIVER QUOTE:
Kenny, "This river is forest-ee, spooky, and wild-er-ness-ee."

CANOE LIVERY:
Northwoods Resort
owners Pam & Ed Kuivanen
N7070 Forest Lake Road
(on H-03, 2 miles south of M28)
Au Train Mi 49806
Phone (906) 892-8114
website www.northwoodsresort.net

Au Train River

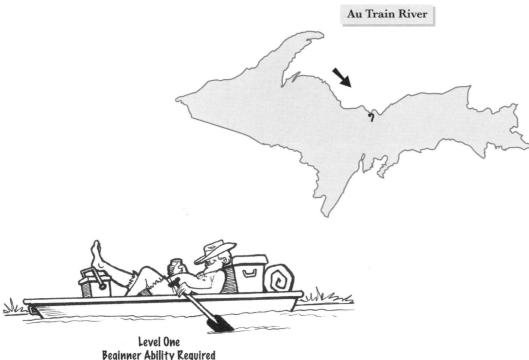

Level One
Beginner Ability Required

THE BACKGROUND: AU TRAIN RIVER

The AuTrain River was a pleasant surprise. We had heard from a number of people that this river was slow and, since we'd just experienced the excitement of the Ford and the Escanaba rapids, we might find the AuTrain a bit boring. Instead of boring, the AuTrain was fun in a different form. Kenny Umphrey and I found the river to be scenic, quiet, and just a bit eerie (as Kenny stated, "this river is forest-ee, spooky, and wild-er-ness-ee"). Some of the eerie feel was due to the large number of uprooted trees seen throughout our ride (as if Mothra and Godzilla had a battle royale along the riverside), a testament to the power and the unpredictable nature of Lake Superior, only 1 mile to the north.

The numerous high banks provide excellent break or camp opportunities, and the many locations where the river is shallow with a sandy river floor free of obstacles make this a class "AAA" Frisbee river.

Although the current is slow, there are reasons for caution. The first is that there are some spots where the water is over 6' deep (at least early in the season, as it was during our mid-May trip). Because of this, life jackets, especially for the kids, would be a good idea. Secondly, in the marshy areas you could get temporarily lost. Where the river splits in two there can be confusion about which split to follow (i.e. which is the main body of the river?). When in doubt, stop paddling. If you still have current behind you, even if you've strayed off the main body you'll soon be reunited with it. If you stop your paddling and there's no current pushing you forward, simply turn around and rejoin the main body.

An AuTrain River bonus: Northwood's rental cost per canoe was the lowest that I've seen in Michigan, on average 30% below the usual canoe livery rental charge.

THE RIVER: PADDLING THE AUTRAIN

The total time of our float down the AuTrain was 1 hour and 45 minutes. To begin the trip, put in at Forest Lake Road's (H-03) southern bridge. There is camping but no toilets on this stretch.

As we put in, the river is 30' wide and over-your-head deep. Just past the 1st bend, the river shallows to 2' deep, returning to over-your-head deep by the 3rd bend.

6 min. in / 1 hr. 39 min. to go: we come upon our 1st island, passable both to the right and to the left. Stay left for faster current and fewer obstacles to negotiate. Water is 3' deep.

11 min. in / 1 hr. 34 min. to go: river makes a big bend right, an ideal Frisbee break area (there will be many today): 50' across, 2' deep, minimal river floor obstacles (i.e. an absence of tree roots, sunken logs, rocks).

15 min. in / 1 hr. 30 min. to go: dead tree fallen into the river from the right shore blocks 75% of the river. Hug the left bank to float through the 10' opening available to you.

20 min. in / 1 hr. 25 min. to go: scraggly-looking island on the river. Just downstream there's a hill on the right bank on which several 15' or larger dead birch trees lay. As the river bends left, you paddle next to a small, grassy island.

23 min. in / 1 hr. 22 min. to go: very long island on the left. Stay to the right. If you float left around the island, fallen trees across the water will force a portage. A blue heron flies nearby, and will be our companion on and off for the next 45 minutes.

27 min. in / 1 hr. 18 min. to go: the river gives you an option to canoe right or left. We suggest that you float left. You'll then paddle by a small sandy slope, a good break spot with space to pull your canoe up, with flat ground on the sandy slope's top. This break or camp spot is the first of several such spots, referred to locally as the high banks.

30 min. in / 1 hr. 15 min. to go: around the right bend is another high banks location, with a 15' wide sandy slope with grassy hillside bookends. This looks to be a fine camping area, marked by a U.S. Forest Service sign visible from the river.

37 min. in / 1 hr. 8 min. to go: the Au Train becomes very marshy, sprinkled with cattails all around. It is hard to determine which way the river goes. Stay to the right, going right around the fallen tree.

41 min. in / 1 hr. 4 min. to go: nice driftwood as the river bends right, followed by a long straightaway. Trees in the distance resemble a green mountain range.

43 min. in / 1 hr. 2 min. to go: just beyond a marshy creek on the right, a fallen tree blocks the entire river. The tree lays parallel above the water, with a number of its branches hanging down into the river. During our mid-May float, the tree trunk was 3' above the water line. Approach the tree very slowly. Right in the middle of the river, there is room between the branches that you can squeeze between. Lean back in the canoe, grab the branches, and pull yourself through.

48 min. in / 57 min. to go: high banks are on the right shore, with its hillside a home to 5 large trees pulled out of the ground so that their roots are exposed (maybe Godzilla and Mothra were here!). The river is shallow near the opposite shore as the river bends left.

51 min. in / 54 min. to go: as you paddle down a long straightaway, on the right you'll pass a wide lagoon and then high banks. At the downstream end of these high banks, the sandy slope makes it easy to pull your canoes up to break or camp at the flat ground above. Past camping evidence can be seen from the river.

Kenny Sez: "This river is sweet, and so's Maple Surple"

58 min. in / 47 min. to go: as the river bends right, on the left shore a very large tree has been uprooted, and you're facing the tree bottom.

At the end of the straightaway is a 2nd large uprooted tree lying on its side, with its bottom roots standing 12' tall.

1 hr. in / 45 min. to go: when you pass the little grassy island on your left, and see a nice looking piece of driftwood on the right, there's 45 minutes left in your ride. 2 minutes beyond is a large island populated with many bushes and tall trees. Although passing the island on the right seems the most obvious was to go, taking the left is a fine option: not only is there plenty of water going left, there is also an attractive sandy break spot going that way. Should you go right and then decide you want to paddle to the sandy break spot on the left, there's a small waterway that splits the island and allows you to do so. Whether you go left or right, you'll reconnect within 2 minutes of the split. Just beyond lies a very tiny island that offers a nice sandy lip for pullovers.

1 hr. 9 min. in / 36 min. to go: at the right is a large lagoon. At the end of the straightaway, high banks are visible. As the river bends left, on the right shore is a high banks sandy slope with a U.S. Forest Service sign visible from our canoes. Many trees show evidence that this is a favorite woodpecker gathering place.

1 hr. 15 min. in / 30 min. to go: big island on the left, you may explore via a left passage. The main river body flows right. Should you take the left around the island, you can visit a high banks with a sitting area that's clearly been enjoyed by others before. The downside of going left is that there is a fallen tree that you'll have to work to pull your canoe over just before you rejoin the river's mainstream.

1 hr. 17 min. in / 28 min. to go: there's a small island and a fine Frisbee area (shallow, no river floor obstacles) as the river bends left.

1 hr. 21 min. in / 24 min. to go: from the right bank, a fallen tree goes completely across the river. By grabbing branches and pulling your way through, there is passage under the tree's middle. Immediately past the fallen tree is the best Frisbee spot of the day: the river is 1' deep, 60' wide, with a gorgeous sandy river bottom.

1 hr. 23 min. in / 22 min. to go: as the river bends left, there's a fine campsite at the high banks on the right. Just beyond these high banks

is an island passable right or left, but a bit congested passing right. There are many cattails near the driftwood. Downstream four minutes a lagoon is on the left and, as the river bends right, yet another nice Frisbee spot.

1 hr. 32 min. in / 13 min. to go: on your left, as the river bends right, sits the final high banks seen on this stretch of the river. This has a very easy-to-climb walk up slope. The slope has the appearance of a big "V" branded into the hillside. Pull your canoe up either the left or right angled sandy pathway.

1 hr. 34 min. in / 11 min. to go: at the "T" in the river, there's a question if you should float right or left. Either way is a safe choice as the river reconnects within 2 minutes.

1 hr. 38 min. in / 7 min. to go: the ride is near the end when, as the river bends right, you see the fine looking log cabin (with nice gazebo and stairs leading to the river) on the left shore, followed shortly by the home with a deck at the river's edge.

Just past the 2nd home lie several islands, creating multiple options about which water path to take around them. The main body of the river flows right. Just beyond these islands is yet another split in the river. You may take any one of 4 ways through these spreads and reconnect within minutes.

1 hour 45 minutes in: the trip ends. Take out on the left, just past the Forest Lake Road northern bridge.

THE TOWN: MUNISING

Detroit Tigers local radio affiliate: WDMJ 1320AM (Marquette)

Munising you say? Aye, a beauty indeed, but she can be a dangerous beauty. Or, to borrow a Vincent Price quote from an old Alice Cooper album, "And here, my prize, the Black Widow. Isn't she lovely? And so deadly."

Isn't she lovely? Just east of Au Train, Munising is located on Lake Superior's south shore, at the mid-point between Houghton-Hancock and Sault Ste. Marie. It is a town surrounded by beauty, ringed on 3 sides by high forested hills, and sitting on a calm bay protected from Lake Superior's occasional fury by Grand Island to Munising's immediate north. Nearby are 17 waterfalls and 5 miles to the town's east lies the western edge of one of Michigan's greatest treasures, the Pictured Rocks National Park.

And so deadly. The number of vessels navigating Lake Superior increased dramatically in the 1840s, spurred on by the discovery of copper riches in the Keweenaw Peninsula and later, iron riches in the Marquette Range. As the vessel activity rose, so did the number of Lake Superior shipwrecks. Arguably, nowhere presented more of a danger than the area around Munising. The Lake Superior coastline bordered by Au Train in the west and Au Sable Point in the east was particularly lethal to shipping. The danger came in many forms: reefs, strong winds coming in off of the sandstone cliffs of Pictured Rocks and Grand Island, thick fog, and the Grand Island's extension at great length into Lake Superior (known as *Gichigami* to the Obijwe tribe). Loss of life from Lake Superior shipwrecks led the Federal government to construct the first of many lighthouses along the big lake's southern shore in 1849. Yesterday's shipwrecks provide a living, and entertainment, for some today: shipwreck tours aboard a glass bottom boat run out of Munising and allow folks to view the remains of 3 shipwrecks.

In addition to contributing to the proliferation of lighthouses, Munising made another major contribution to our great state: in 1922, Munising public works superintendent, Edward Levy, mounted on runners two 10' x 20' retractable wooden wings, and thus Edward had designed the nation's first snowplow.

Sources: Munising Shipwrecks by Frederick Stonehouse, www.munising.com

THE TAVERN: TRAILS END - CHRISTMAS, MI

Once you're off the AuTrain, it's a 9 mile drive to Trails End. Take H03/Forest Lake Rd. north until it ends at M28 and Lake Superior. Follow M28 east and the tavern will be on your left. Trails End is a very comfortable little roadside tavern, the perfect place to relax with a burger and a beer after a fun float down the AuTrain. Trails End has a pool table, a video machine, & a juke box. Pabst in cans and Blatz in bottles are among the beers that they offer. Wood-paneled, Trails End achieves the difficult balance of looking clean, new, and still comfortable.

ESCANABA RIVER
MARQUETTE, MICHIGAN

RIVER SOUNDTRACK:
How High the Moon – Les Paul & Mary Ford
Soul Kitchen - Doors
Big Iron – Marty Robbins
Downtown – Petula Clark
In The Hall Of The Mountain King/Bolero - SRC

CANOE LIVERY:
Uncle Ducky Outfitters
owner Bill Duckwall
434 E. Prospect, Marquette Mi 49855
Phone (906) 228-5447
www.uncleduckyoutfitters.com

RIVER QUOTE:
Jeff, "I had a candy bar in my room last night."
"Kenny, "And that was just her stage name."

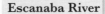

Escanaba River

Level Two
Intermediate Ability Required

THE BACKGROUND: ESCANABA RIVER

Neal Linkon, Jeff Mitchell, Kenny Umphrey, and I embarked on what was advertised to be a 3 hour Escanaba River float. Our put in was at the well-maintained Community Park in Gwinn, with take out planned for the Iron Pin Road access, prior to the Escanaba's junction with its West Branch. The fast mid-May current shortened the actual canoe time to 1 hour and 45 minutes, and every one of those 105 minutes was a real treat. Sunshine, occasional runs of rapids, friendly chatter with the trout fishermen found frequently along our ride, no one was at work, and everyone was in a great mood (there's a shocker, eh?). Maybe Harry McClintock was right, and they hung the jerk that invented work. Whether they did or didn't, there was happily no sign of him on the Escanaba.

Another happy memory of the Escanaba River experience was listening to the stories told by our livery host, Bill Duckwall, aka Uncle Ducky. Bill easily recounts past trips down waterways throughout the Upper Peninsula, in such a way that you'd like to stay and paddle down all of 'em. Now there's an idea.

THE RIVER: PADDLING THE ESCANABA

The total time of our trip was 1 hour and 45 minutes. We put in at the Gwinn Community Park, starting the trip with a 9 minute float down the Escanaba's East Branch until it merges with the main river, the Escanaba Middle Branch. There are no toilets or parks along the journey.

Upon our East Branch put in, we immediately float below the M35 Bridge. The river is 30' wide and 2' deep. 100 yards beyond M35 is a 200' run of light rapids, as the river width tightens from 30' to 20' wide.

8 min. in / 1 hr. 37 min. to go: paddle beneath the white bridge. 1 minute downstream, the Escanaba's East Branch current takes our canoe to the left as the East Branch and our 2 canoes merge with the Middle Branch. We are now officially on the Big Escanaba. At the East Branch junction, the Escanaba is 80' wide and 3' deep.

14 min. in / 1 hr. 31 min. to go: a beautiful cabin on the left gets a twin salute for flying both the Stars & Stripes and the Yooper flags.

17 min. in / 1 hr. 28 min. to go: a small grassy island, 20' long and 10' wide, where the river bends left. 3 minutes beyond and on the left shore sits a home with a garden and sunroom. Just downstream, a big creek merges from the left, across the river from an island.

23 min. in / 1 hr. 22 min. to go: rapids begin as we approach a mighty fine foot

bridge set high above the river. Use caution as just beyond the bridge there are two very large and visible rocks midstream. 30' to the right of these two rocks are two more large, but not quite as visible (depending on water level), rocks that you will not want to meet up with. Hug the right shore to avoid this meeting.

Beyond the foot bridge and these large rocks, 100 yards of calm water followed by rapids run the balance of a long straightaway. Over the next 3 bends, a long stretch of rapids is followed by a 100 to 200 yard stretch of quiet water, then rapids again, and so on.

34 min. in / 1 hr. 11 min. to go: calm water takes over, as the river widens slightly to 90' across with a depth of 3'.

45 min. in / 1 hr. to go: you'll know that there's 1 hour of your ride remaining when you see the horse fence on the left bank.

47 min. in / 58 min. to go: a small gray viewing stand is on the left shore.

51 min. in / 54 min. to go: a 500' long very light rapids run.

> *Kenny Sez:* *"Taking the shortest route is kinda like painless dentistry.*
> *It may sound good before it happens, but …"*

58 min. in / 47 min. to go: as the Escanaba bends left, there's a 120' rapids run, just fast enough to get your interest.

1 hr. 16 min. in / 29 min. to go: a small, but loud, stream merges from the right.

1 hr. 23 min. in / 22 min. to go: a large, long tangle of driftwood sits near the right shore.

1 hr. 30 min. in / 15 min. to go: good looking limestone chimney and log cabin, right shore.

1 hr. 36 min. in / 9 min. to go: island sits on the left side of the Escanaba.

1 hr. 42 min. in / 3 min. to go: we float beneath the power lines. The take out point is in sight, around the next bend, ahead on the left.

1 hr. 45 min. in: the ride ends on the left bank at the Iron Pin Road access.

THE TOWN: MARQUETTE

Detroit Tigers local radio affiliate: WDMJ 1320 AM (Marquette).

Marquette is home to the Northern Michigan University Wildcats ("For Northern's glory, Fight for the green and gold"). The town is named after the French missionary and river explorer, Father Jacques Marquette, who visited the area in the late-1600s. Marquette became a village in 1859, and today is one of the Upper Peninsula's largest cities. Its location on Lake Superior made it an ideal shipping center for the nearby iron ore ranges. The 1859 opening of the first dock to ship iron ore from the Marquette Range to all over the U.S. made the town the U.P.'s commercial center (although it's iron ore shipments were soon surpassed by Escanaba), and the jobs created brought to Marquette Italians, Finns, Scandinavians, French, Cornish (and their pasties), Irish, and Germans.

One of the descendants of those Germans was John Voelker, a Michigan treasure. John was a graduate of Northern Michigan University and the University of Michigan's law school, lawyer, Michigan Supreme Court Justice, fly fisherman, writer, a man who loved nature and the great outdoors, especially those found in the Upper Peninsula. John's affection for the U.P., and concern for its over-development,

was legendary. When, in 1957, John was asked to attend the official ceremony to open the Mackinac Bridge, he declined, explaining that this would conflict with his duties as head of the "bomb the bridge" committee (most believe that John was kidding). Another Voelkerism reflected his concern about the despoiling of his beloved U.P.: "Is our world becoming hopelessly divided into two kinds of people, those who love trees and those who love logs?"

Outside of Michigan, John is likely best known as the author of *Anatomy of a Murder*, the same book being read by Ringo during the Beatles' movie, *Hard Day's Night*. John wrote the book under his pen name of Robert Traver. The book is based on an actual crime committed in Big Bay, 40 minutes to the northwest of Marquette, & the subsequent 1952 murder trial in which John Voelker was the defense attorney. In 1959, a movie was made about the book, directed by Otto Preminger, music by Duke Ellington, with Jimmy Stewart playing the role of

John as the defense attorney. The movie brought a great deal of notoriety to both Voelker and Marquette.

Type "Anatomy of a Murder" into your search engine, then click on the first entry and you can watch a 1959 promotional video for the movie. In a courtroom setting, Otto Preminger swears in the movie's stars (Jimmy Stewart, Lee Remick, Ben Gazzara, George C. Scott, among others), Duke Ellington, and John Voelker himself. It's great fun to watch!

Many toasts have been made along the Fox and the Manistique Rivers, and certainly in many other Michigan locales, saluting John Voelker, never more than upon his passing in 1991. Quoted from along many river trips is John's "Testament of a Fisherman". I'll take the liberty to substitute canoeing for fishing, but the spirit remains the same.

"I fish because I love to; because I love the environs where trout are found, which are inevitably beautiful, and hate the environs where crowds of people are found, which are invariably ugly; because of all the television commercials, cocktail parties, and assorted social posturing I thus escape; because, in a world where most men seem to spend their lives doing things they hate, my fishing is at once an endless source of delight and an act of small rebellion; because trout do not lie or cheat and cannot be bought or bribed or impressed by power, but respond only to quietude and humility and endless patience; because I suspect that men are going along this way for the last time, and I for one don't want to waste the trip; because mercifully there are no telephones on trout waters; because only in the woods can I find solitude without loneliness; because bourbon out of an old tin cup always tastes better out there; because maybe one day I will catch a mermaid; and, finally, not because I regard fishing as being so terribly important but because I suspect that so many of the other concerns of men are equally unimportant – and not nearly so much fun."

Sources: old newspaper articles, Michigan by Bruce Catton, Anatomy of a Murder web site.

THE TAVERN: WOODEN NICKEL - MARQUETTE

Small and intimate, the Wooden Nickel is your basement bar with 20 friends, 20 cases of Pabst, with the Door's Soul Kitchen playing in the background. The Nickel claims to be Michigan's oldest bar, and with both Pabst and Blatz longnecks available, it's an easy mental exercise to imagine that it's true. One pool table is squeezed in against the back wall. Hundreds of photos of the famous, both those nationally and those only inside these 4 walls, provide the wall decor. Jack "here's Johnny!" Torrence, Honest Abe, Carl "total consciousness" Spackler, and Johnny Cash all look very much at home here. Great juke box! Sawdust covers the odd historical moments within her walls, as well as the floor. Rumored by locals to have mellowed a bit from its era of pirates and bikers…Close your eyes, inhale, and notice that the scent of the Nickel is a bit like your favorite 1974 album. Classic beer signs catch your eye in every direction, but the best sign is the one behind the bar, stating one of the Wooden Nickel's few rules: "Anyone who buys for a minor will be barred for life, shot, then shot again."

FORD RIVER
ESCANABA, MICHIGAN

RIVER SOUNDTRACK:
Hotel Yorba – White Stripes
Lillie Mae – Smiley Lewis
The Pasty Song – Derek Wright
Travelin' Shoes – Mountain Heart
Margaritaville – Jimmy Buffett

CANOE LIVERY:
Mr. Rental
owner Rich McInerney
627 Stephenson Ave, Escanaba, Mi. 49829
Phone (906) 789-7776 or (866) 906-7776
No website

RIVER QUOTE:
Kenny "How do you get down from an elephant? You don't. You get down from a duck."

Ford River

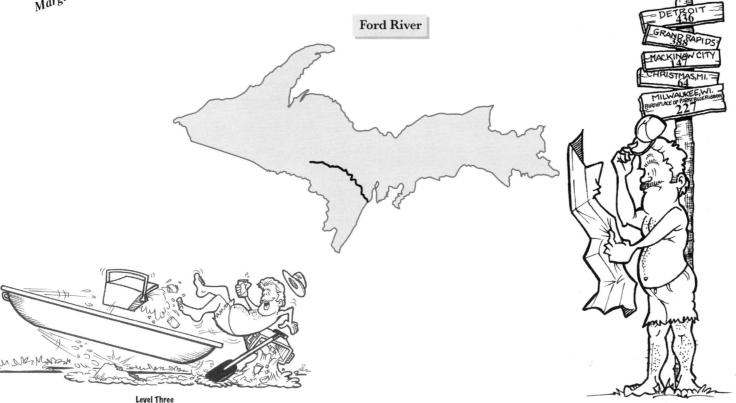

Level Three
Veteran Ability Required

THE BACKGROUND: FORD RIVER

Trails.com describes the Ford River as "an ideal springtime destination for winter-weary canoeists with an itch to scratch." The Ford River 4, Neal Linkon, Jeff Mitchell, Ken Umphrey, and I, found that description to be perfect and the Ford to be a wonderful mid-May adventure. Liery owner Rich McInerney grew up on the Ford and was a helpful source as we planned our trip. The Ford is a stream-fed, seasonal river, reaching its ideal depth during the period from late-April through early-June. By mid-June, the river is generally so low as to force you to get out of your canoe and walk it through many spots. Not an enjoyable prospect. If you cannot get on the Ford before early-June, you'll want to wait until right after a heavy rain or take the trip on a different year.

The evening before our canoeing adventure, we stayed at the historic, charming, and very affordable House of Ludington hotel. The HOL was built in 1864, houses Michigan's 1st glass-enclosed elevator, along with a fine little Irish pub, and has provided lodging for, among many others, John Sousa, Henry Ford, Prince Bertil of Sweden, Cornelius Vanderbilt Jr., Guy Lombardo, Jimmy Hoffa, Johnny Cash, and George Gobel (*Peter Marshall*: true or false, a pea can last as long as 5,000 years; *George Gobel*: Boy, it sure seems that way sometimes). Proprietors Ed & Suzell were gracious hosts, and the hotel's location near the Sand Point Lighthouse, on the south shore of Little Bay de Noc and on the north shore of Green Bay, make it a great place for a morning walk or jog.

THE RIVER: PADDLING THE FORD

The total time of our trip was 2 hours and 45 minutes. We put in at 1 Road, better known to those nearby as the Hyde Cut Across. There are no parks or toilets along the way.

The Ford adventure starts 50' upstream from the Hyde Bridge. At our put in, the river is running 1' deep and 70' across, with a current speed of medium-fast. The river floor is all rock.

2 min. in / 2 hrs 43 min. to go: a fun chop develops with some bottom-skimming, running for several minutes.

7 min. in / 2 hr. 38 min. to go: float beneath a passenger car (converted railroad) bridge. Many rocks just past the bridge cause quite a bit of bumping and bouncing. We begin to see Canadian Geese, our companions throughout the trip.

8 min. in / 2 hr. 37 min. to go: we see our first island, suggest passing on the left as the right is very shallow. If you do go right, hug the right shore or you'll bottom out. Just beyond the island is a 2.5-3 minutes long straightaway rapids run, choppy and fun. The river depth here is 2'. After the rapids, the river slows and deepens to 3'.

18 min. in / 2 hr. 27 min. to go: a pretty cool-looking observation post, or gazebo, is on the left bank. It's built around a tall tree that goes through the bottom and the top of the gazebo. Beware the big rock in the middle of the river, or while you're gazebo-gazing it'll get you.

20 min. in / 2 hr. 25 min. to go: 2nd island today, very flat and heavily populated with reeds and a long piece of driftwood. Passable both right & left, with the river wider going right.

22 min. in / 2 hr. 23 min. to go: as the Ford bends right, a creek flowing in from the left adds sufficient volume to the river to deepen it to 4'.

32 min. in / 2 hr. 13 min. to go: float beneath a railroad bridge, followed 50' downstream by the Highway 41 & 2 Bridge.

38 min. in / 2 hr. 7 min. to go: 60' long island on the river's left is preceded by a 100' run of very light rapids.

48 min. in / 1 hr. 57 min. to go: break time! A nice-looking creek, 15' wide at its mouth, merges from the right shore. The elevated high ground at this river-creek junction, with its nice sitting log, makes a fine break or camping spot. The creek winds beautifully as it approaches the Ford, and is worth exploring with a walk either up the creek or along the adjacent elevated high ground.

50 min. in / 1 hr. 55 min. to go: encounter a 100' choppy run as the river bends left. Even during the Ford's peaceful moments (i.e. absent chop/rapids/waves) the current is quick!
3 minutes downstream, around the right bend and at a home with a beautiful deck, we enjoy a nice 200' rapids run.

56 min. in / 1 hr. 49 min. to go: a new rapids run begins at the start of a very long straight-away. Choppy water is seen the entire length of this one-quarter mile straightaway, with thick woods on both banks (great stretch!). Large rocks are dotted throughout this five minute run, forcing you to make quick decisions, and your back stiffens as you weave your way around and through the obstacle course. Waves came over the top of our canoe at times. After a brief 200' run of calm water, as we go to the left of an approaching island, the river kicks up again, shallow and choppy. In high water, this is the start of over a 1 mile run of class 2 rapids.

Just past this island, as the river bends left, we pass another much smaller island, passable either left or right (the main body of the river flows right).

1 hr. 8 min. in / 1 hr. 37 min. to go: *consider a left or right shore portage!* Immediately before a you float under a foot bridge, you encounter a brief stretch of class 2-3 rapids. This a short drop of intense water where the river narrows. Complicating your efforts is an angled ledge, running from the right shore to the middle of the river. Jeff and Neal stayed left – and upright – through this rough water. Kenny and I went slightly right- center and, as we were working our way to the calmer water along the right shore, our canoe was caught on the angled ledge. We could not stop our canoe from turning sideways, exposing the right side of our boat to the crashing, on-coming waves, and leaving us too vulnerable to stay upright in the intense rapids. Avoid the ledge.

Immediately downstream from the ledge, a series of very large rocks are scattered throughout the river. Approach as slowly as you can and pick your way through.

1 hr. 16 min. in / 1 hr. 29 min. to go: enjoyable little rapids run as the river bends right.

1 hr. 23 min. in / 1 hr. 22 min. to go: you're at the halfway point when, at the end of a long straightaway, where the river bends left, you see a beige home with a 2nd floor balcony.

Kenny Sez: "I was asked for some words of wisdom. 64 years experience and I got nothin' (sigh)"

1 hr. 27 min. in / 1 hr. 18 min. to go: begin a 3-minute run of light rapids, very shallow with bottom-skimming and large rocks dotting the run. At the end of this run is an extremely large (4' wide) rock, visible well above the river's surface on the right side of the Ford.
A small island lies on a straightaway just beyond this large rock. Stay far right as there are large, hidden rocks on the left and center approaches to the island.

For the next 20 minutes downstream from this island, you'll enjoy a very spirited and choppy rapids run. Waves crash into our canoe as we paddle through a long-running rock garden. The Michigamme River on steroids comes to mind.

1 hr. 40 min. in / 1 hr. 5 min. to go: an island appears. If you pass on the right, you'll see the river split around yet another island. If you pass this second island on the right, beware of a treacherous drop to the river.

1 hr. 47 min. in / 58 min. to go: begins a series of 6 islands, at times separated by only 10'.

1 hr. 50 min. in / 55 min. to go: the 20 minute rapids run ends. The river bottom changes from stone to sand and the Ford now seems like a completely different river. Extreme peacefulness overtakes the river, the water deepens to 4', and all is very quiet except for the birds who are suddenly singing all around us. Homes begin to appear in numbers, primarily on the right shore. Several eagles fly above us over the next several minutes.

2 hrs 10 min. in / 35 min. to go: a tree leaning over the river from the right shore supports two bat houses. 3 minutes downstream, the river widens to 120' across.

2 hrs 17 min. in / 28 min. to go: huge, flat rock near the left bank covers half of the river.
This squeezes the water's flow, creating a rapids that runs for several bends. The rocky river bottom returns, average water depth is now 1', with some shallower areas causing bottom-skimming.

2 hrs 22 min. in / 23 min. to go: a creek merges from the right, 15' wide at its mouth.

2 hrs 24 min. in / 21 min. to go: an impressive seawall constructed of logs supports the right bank, dissected by a creek entering from the right. This creek adds enough volume to the river so that the water deepens to 2' and the rapids come to an end. The river bottom is once again sandy. An expensive and fine-looking home sits on the right bank above the log seawall. We are told that the wall and the home are on Indian land. "Slow no wake" signs begin to appear.

2 hrs 28 min. in / 17 min. to go: big creek merges from the left, and two homes sit along the creek's shore just before it joins with the Ford. Just downstream, an island is on the right side of the river.

2 hours 45 minutes in: the trip ends. Take out on the left just past the Highway 35 Bridge.

THE TOWN: ESCANABA

Detroit Tigers local radio affiliate: WDKJ 1320AM (Marquette)

Portable beef stew, folded over in a baked, golden brown, pie dough… mmm, mmm…What's more Upper Peninsula than the pasty (pronounced "pass-tee")? Escanaba was born, and pasties introduced to America, as a by product of the Keweenaw Peninsula 1860s iron ore boom. Upon the discovery of what seemed to be unlimited quantities of iron ore, veterans of copper mining in England – referred to as "Cousin Jacks" – came literally by the boatload to make it rich in the iron ore mines of the western U.P. These English brought with them the staple of their British mining diet: the handy- to-eat-on-the-job Cornish pasty.

In order to transport Keweenaw iron ore to the blast furnaces populating towns along the northwest shore of the Lower Peninsula, rail lines were laid from the iron ranges in Marquette and Menominee to the area of the little Bay de Noc, one of the best deep water ports on the entire Great Lakes. From this area, which became Escanaba, the iron was loaded on to steamers bound for those Lower Peninsula blast furnaces. As a major lake port, Escanaba was the shipping point for lumber & fish, but its greatest fame was in transporting iron ore. Escanaba became known to all as "The Iron Port of the World". Today, Escanaba still serves as a major iron ore port, shipping to Chicago, Milwaukee, Green Bay and other locations in the Midwest.

Research for the origin of the name "Escanaba" shows two claims. The first is that the name is derived from the Indian word meaning "land of the Red Buck", a reference to a well-known buck and deer trail that cut through a popular hunting ground just north of town. The second claim is that, in the 1830s the area was known as Flat Rock, and "Escowanaba" is the Nokay Indian word for *flat rock*, an accurate description of the nearby Escanaba River bed.

The area's earliest European inhabitants, circa 1830s, were English, French, Italian, and Scandinavian. These town folk, as well as the traveling iron ore merchants & sailors, apparently developed a powerful thirst: by 1860 nearly every other Ludington Street (Escanaba's main thoroughfare) business was a saloon. By 1905 there were a total of 103 saloons in Escanaba where, it is assumed, the 1893 World's Fair blue ribbon winning beer (aka Pabst) was a popular seller.

Sources: Michigan by Bruce Canton, Michigan Yesterday & Today by Ferris Lewis, Delta County Historical Society, Escanaba park plaques

THE TAVERN: THE FORD RIVER PUB

As soon as you depart the river access lot and enter Highway 35, turn right. The Ford River Pub will be on your left, not even 100 yards away, located in (as noted on the pub menu) beautiful downtown Ford River. The FRB is home to very friendly proprietors, Kim and Matt, and its regulars. Smiles, stories, jokes, and good feelings surrounded us, and *Margaritaville* was playing when we came through the door. We've clearly come to the right place. Bob, very much a regular, bought us each a beer within 5 minutes of our walking in. Pabst is available in cans only, but we're pleasantly surprised with the availability of Blatz longnecks! Besides its warmth extended to all who enter, the FRP has a great juke box, 2 pool tables, darts, and 3 video games to while away your time. The Ford River Pub is melt-right-in-comfortable.

TAHQUAMENON RIVER
PARADISE, MICHIGAN

CANOE LIVERY: The Woods
owners Ken Orlang
P.O. Box 536, Newberry MI 49868
Ph (906) 203-7624
no website
The Woods is located exactly 13 miles north of
Newberry on M-123. Driving north from Newberry
on M-123, the entrance to The Woods will be on
your right.

RIVER SOUNDTRACK:
Paradise – John Prine
Mosquitoes, Gnats, & No-See-Ems – Yard Dogs
I Put A Spell On You – Creedence Clearwater
Revival
Sleepy Lagoon – Platters
Mosquito Song – Queens Of The Stone Age
Burning Love – Elvis
(memorializing the 2007 area fire, Michigan's 3rd
largest ever)

RIVER QUOTE:
Doc, *"I never met a river that I didn't like"*

Tahquamenon River

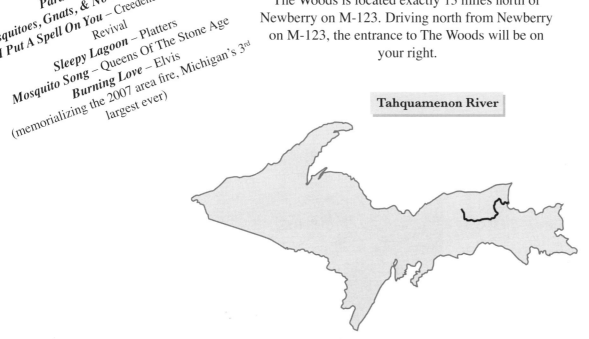

Level One
Beginner Ability Required

THE BACKGROUND: TAHQUAMENON RIVER

The Tahquamenon is mentioned in W.W. Longfellow's poem "Hiawatha"

Give me of your bark, O Birch-tree! Of your yellow bark, O Birch tree!
Growing by the rushing river, Tall and stately in the valley
I a light canoe will build me, Build a swift Cheemaun for sailing,
That shall float on the river, Like a yellow leaf in Autumn,
Like a yellow water lily!
Thus aloud cried Hiawatha, In the solitary forest,
By the rushing Taquamenaw, When the birds were singing gaily,
In the Moon of Leaves were singing, And the sun, from sleep awaking,
Started up and said, "Behold me! Gheezis, the great sun, behold me!

The Tahquamenon River is blessed with lagoons (14 viewed on today's suggested trip) and mosquitoes (numbered to infinity, at least in mid-June, seems the right estimate). Our original plan called for canoeing with the Tahquamenon General Store & Canoe Rental folks,

Gene & Sheri McLellen, on the only trip that they offered: a 17-mile float starting at the base of the Lower Falls (which would provide us with a beautiful view of the Falls) and taking out where the river ends at Whitefish Bay. Not realizing how slow this river flows, we had estimated that the 17 miles would take 6 hours at most.

Arriving at Gene & Sheri's livery, the weather was a wet 49 degrees and it was raining the afore-mentioned mosquitoes. Gene and Sheri provided us with one other handy piece of information: this 17-mile stretch of the river is very slow, and paddling it at a nice, steady pace may take us up to 8 hours or longer. They also said that, as much as they'd like to take our money, they don't think that 8 hours or so on a rainy, mosquito day like today would be an enjoyable one for us, and suggested that we come back during another warmer, drier time to run the 17 miles (a very classy move on the part of the McLellens). They also suggested that, since we strongly desired to get into a boat today, that we take a much shorter trip with a competitor (even classier), The Woods. Arriving at The Woods, owner Ken similarly warned us about the skeeters out on the river, but with a much shorter 2-3 hour trip, we were willing to forge ahead.

The mosquito-fightin', Tahquamenon River runners were Mister P Pienta, Toni LaPorte, Gomie Carroll, Kanoo Kenny Umphrey, Tomquamenon Holbrook, Maggie, and me.

Side note: the 17-mile Tahquamenon River trip offered by the McLellens, runs from the base of the Lower Falls to Whitefish Bay, and is the setting for an annual September river race event known as the Wilderness Canoe Race. The event is hosted by the Michigan Canoe Racing Association and the Paradise Chamber of Commerce.

THE RIVER: PADDLING THE TAHQUAMENON

The suggested trip runs 2 hours and 50 minutes, with the put in at the M-123 Bridge, behind the Tahquamenon River Logging Museum, and 1 mile to the north of Newberry. From here, the river runs straight east until the take out at McPhee's Landing at County Road 462. There will be no campgrounds and no toilets on today's ride.

As this stretch begins, you float under the M-123 Bridge. The river is 3' deep and 35' wide. These dimensions will change little today. Beyond the bridge is a small waterfall on the right.

5 min. in / 2 hr. 45 min. to go: On your left, a sandy bank precedes a boat launch. 3 minutes downstream, a creek with a good current behind it merges from your right.

17 min. in / 2 hr. 33 min. to go: The first of 14 lagoons you will see today, sits on the left, 30' wide and 30' deep. 3 minutes later, as the river bends left another lagoon sits on the right.

24 min. in / 2 hr. 26 min. to go: A creek merges from the left. 3 minutes downstream, the lagoon on the right runs fairly deep into the marshland. Crack researcher Tom-quamenon suggests that this river be measured not in feet, but rather by cans of Deet.

37 min. in / 2 hrs 13 min. to go: As the river bends left, a creek of some size joins the river from the right. Near the merger, a bat house sits on a log.

1 hr. 8 min. in / 1 hr. 42 min. to go: A small lagoon on the right is where the river bends to the left. 100 yards downstream is flat ground on the right that would make a fine spot for a river break. Since we had Gomie with us, perhaps some buck dancing at this break spot would be in order. Buck dancing is an old time southern dance, kind of like clogging, in which the legs are kicking up a storm while there's not too much movement above the waist. And it don't get much better 'n watching Gomie doing the storm kicking! You can view a great exhibition of buck dancing (almost as good as Gomie's) by typing "buck dancing" into your search engine and watch Emmylou Harris getting jiggy with it.

1 hr. 10 min. in / 1 hr. 40 min. to go: The river bends right where a large creek merges from the left. The creek is large enough that, when viewed on the approach, there's some doubt about whether or not the creek is the river itself. The area has grown increasingly marshy. Around the next bend lies yet another lagoon.

1 hr. 20 min. in / 1 hr. 30 min. to go: At the end of a long straightaway, the river flows left where a lagoon is on the right. At the river bend, a fallen tree blocks all but a small opening along the left shore.

Kenny Sez: *"A little drizzle is better than a little drool"*

1 hr. 28 min. in / 1 hr. 22 min. to go: Down a straightaway, the lagoon on the left is 80' wide, twice the width of the river. Float by 2 more lagoons over the next 5 minutes.
The mosquito bites are clouding our thinking, evident by the question asked, "Is beeralope a fruit?" (is there any doubt?)

2 hrs in / 50 min. to go: The river bends right where a lagoon lies left. Downstream five minutes is a lagoon on the right. 3 minutes further downstream, a tiny canal connects the Tahquamenon with a large pond on the right. It is here that Maggie utters the words that define her day, "The mosquito net headgear is the difference between heaven and hell. The river is divided into B.H. (before the hat) and A.H. (after the hat). The A.H. is pronounced "ahhh…" as in blessed relief.

2 hrs 20 min. in / 30 min. to go: 8 minutes beyond lagoon number 12, and where the river bends right, there is a steep clay incline on the left bank. 5' up the incline is flat ground, but the clay is too slippery on a wet day to climb easily. 100 yards downstream is a friendlier slope on the left shore, a location where it's easy to pull the boats up for a break. The mosquitoes agree and break with us. This is a state boat launch put in point.

2 hrs 34 min. in / 16 min. to go: Lagoon number 13 is spotted with number 14 just five minutes downstream. These are the final two lagoons seen today.

2 hrs 46 min. in / 4 min. to go: A tree fallen from the left shore blocks all but a 10' gap along the right bank. You are 2 minutes from the trip's end when you pass the ruins of a dock on your right.

2 hours and 50 minutes and you're in at McPhee's Landing. The mosquito buffet is at an end until the next victims arrive. Exit on the right.

THE TOWN: PARADISE

Detroit Tigers local radio affiliate: WNBY 1450 AM (Newberry)

There are two seasons in Paradise: swatting and shoveling. So proclaims a T-shirt referring to the town's abundance of skeeters (many) and snow (much). In addition to prodigious quantities of the two, Paradise is home to Whitefish Point with its Shipwreck Museum, and to Michigan's largest state park, Tahquamenon Falls.

The Great Lakes holds enough water to cover the entire United States in 9.5' of water.

17 miles northwest of Whitefish Point is where the 29 men of the Edmund Fitzgerald lost their lives on November 10, 1975. The ship was not alone: in the 80 miles along the coast stretching from Whitefish Point west to Pictured Rocks, there have been over 300 shipwrecks recorded over the years. This is the cost of conducting shipping in an area where a 200 mile sweep of open water allows terrible storms to build up, combined with poor visibility and heavy traffic converging into tight shipping lanes. These factors have contributed to Whitefish Point earning the title "Graveyard of the Great Lakes".

On November 10, 1975, Lake Superior was caught in the worst storm seen by veteran sailors in over 30 years. Winds gusted to 96 miles an hour with waves cresting at 30' high. The final transmission from the *Edmund Fitzgerald,* "we are holding our own".

The European discovery of Lake Superior is considered to have occurred in 1621, and is credited to the French explorer Etienne Brule. Early explorers had heard tales of a great northern sea far above Lake Huron. What they believed would be a route to the

Orient turned out to be the largest, deepest and coldest fresh water lake in the world. Also, a dangerous lake: all told, over 550 shipwrecks have taken place on Lake Superior.

Since 1975, the *Fitzgerald* has laid at the bottom of Lake Superior, in water 535' deep, 17 miles from Whitefish Point. In 1995, twenty years after the good ship and crew wrecked, surviving family members of the ship's crew, along with the Great Lakes Shipwreck Historical Society, Canadian Navy and the National Geographic Society, raised the ship's bell to honor the 29 lost men.

To the west of Whitefish Bay is Tahquamenon Falls, famous for the magnificent Upper Falls. Measured at 200' wide and with a vertical drop of almost 50', the Upper Falls is the second largest waterfall east of the Mississippi River. Only Niagara Falls is larger. During the extremely dry summer of 2007, the Upper Falls split into two falls, exposing the sandstone rock in the Falls' center, and leaving it looking a bit like Darren McCarty's gap-toothed smile.

4 miles downstream from the Upper Falls is the Lower Falls. Here the Tahquamenon River splits in two as it flows around an island, breaking into a series of 5 smaller falls, as beautiful in their own way as the Upper Falls.

Sources: www.michigan.gov/dnr, www.uppermichiganwaterfalls.com, Great Lakes Shipwreck Museum. www.exploringthenorth.com

THE TAVERNS: YUKON INN & TAHQUAMENON FALLS BREWERY & PUB

In Paradise, located at the junction where the road to Whitefish Point splits with the road to Tahquamenon Falls, sits the log cabin-styled Yukon Inn. Built in the 1930s, the Yukon has a sign outside that tells you that you are walking into the "Friendliest Bar In The North". Our night at the tavern did not indicate otherwise. The Yukon has a side room with 8 video games, and a juke box in the main room. The main room is also where one can purchase and enjoy the bar's signature dish, "The Yukonburger": a third-pound of ground beef, a layer of bacon, a layer of ham, 2 pieces of cheese, all served on a sesame seed bun. The Yukonburger tasted good enough to tempt a semi-vegetarian in our group to have sweet desires of a second one. A review of the balance of the menu prompted a friend to comment, "If it's not fried, it's not here". If there's room in your luggage, bring along an extra artery. And, oh yes, Pabst Blue Ribbon Beer was offered to the Yukon's patrons, always a sure sign of quality.

There's another nearby tavern that has a location sure to keep a steady flow of traffic through its doors: The Tahquamenon Falls Brewery & Pub, located next to the parking lot in the Tahquamenon Falls State Park. The love of the Tahquamenon River & the Falls, and the desire to allow as many people as possible to enjoy both, led Jack and Mimi Barrett to bestow the gift of land adjacent to the Falls to the DNR. Jack & Mimi frequently canoed from their Newberry home to the base of the Falls, during a time when the Falls were accessible only by boat. The Barretts worked to make a road to the Falls a reality, then deeded the land to the DNR with the requirement that (1) the

land be used for a state park and (2) that the park road and parking lot would end .75 mile from the Falls, leaving the forest next to the Falls untouched. Within the land deeded to the state, Jack and Mimi kept 3 acres for themselves. On these 3 acres in 1950, they built a replica of one of the Barrett Logging Company camps, Camp 33. The camp was so named as it was the 33rd logging camp the Barrett Co. constructed. The plan was to allow this replica camp to be a place where Falls visitors could have a bite & a drink. In the 1990s, Jack & Mimi's grandkids rebuilt Camp 33 into the structure that visitors see today, one that houses The Tahquamenon Falls Brewery & Pub – and the Camp 33 Gift Shop. I believe that this is where Paul Harvey tells us that "now we know…"

Sources: www.superiorsights.com

RIVERS LESS PADDLED IN LOWER MICHIGAN

BEAR RIVER PETOSKEY, MICHIGAN

RIVER SOUNDTRACK:
The Great Gig In The Sky – Pink Floyd
(Richard Wright tribute)
When My Rowboat Comes In – Stevie
Goodman
Blue Skies – Willie Nelson
God's Own Drunk – Jimmy Buffett
Moon River – Andy Williams

CANOE LIVERY:
Bear River Canoe Livery
owners Karen & Dave Fettig
2517 McDougal, Petoskey, Mi. 49770.
Phone (231) 347-9038 or (231) 838-4141
no website.
Directions: US31 South to Division (just south of
the Bay View G.C.) & turn left. Take Division until
it ends, turn right on Atkin. Follow Atkin to just past
the top of the hill and turn left at McDougall. The
livery will be on your right in one & one-half mile.

RIVER QUOTE
Livery owner Dave's final words of wisdom
as he dropped us off at the riverside: "Go that
way"

Level One
Beginner Ability Required

Bear River

THE BACKGROUND: BEAR RIVER

I called Maggie when our Bear River trip was finished, and she asked me "How was the river?" I said "It was beautiful." When Maggie told me that I always say that, I concluded that perhaps I should have been added the words "the most" in front of beautiful. Kanoo Kenny Umphrey, Tommy Holbrook, and I were awe-struck by the Bear. In honor of the river's name, let's say that we were paw-struck.

On riverfacts.com, it was written that a 1 mile long stretch of the Bear is rated as a class 2 to class 3 rapids. When livery owner Karen was asked if this segment of the river was handled by the livery, she said that, for their customer's safety and for the safety of the livery's equipment, this ride was no longer made available to customers. If you type "Bear River Petoskey Michigan" into your search engine, you can view a You Tube 6 minute plus piece that shows kayakers taking on these rapids. These rapids look like great fun, but <u>not</u> canoeing safe for 99% of folks. Good decision Karen.

THE RIVER: PADDLING THE BEAR

The suggested trip runs 2 hours and 20 minutes, with the put in at County Line Road, also known as Bear River Road. The source of Bear River is Walloon Lake. The river has no major tributaries, and is fed by springs draining the surrounding hills. Bear River has its own set of "spreads", where the river splits, reconnects, and then splits again. You may take any number of little channels, knowing that eventually you will reconnect to the river's main body. These spreads, adding both to the river's beauty and adventure, begin at the 50 minute mark and will run for one half of an hour.

Today, you'll paddle through three culverts. When you float past the first of the 3, there will be 53 minutes left in your ride. The trip ends at the canoe livery, just moments after floating through the final set of culverts. Along this 2 hour and 20 minute stretch of the Bear River, there are no maintained campgrounds and there are no toilets.

The river is shallow and rocky at the County Line Road Bridge put in, 40' across from shore to shore, and moving slowly. Within 2 bends the river is 4' deep. As soon as you begin, a creek flows into the river from the right, the first of many creeks that you will see today. This beginning segment of the Bear is similar in appearance to the stretch of the U.P.'s Fox river 2 hours upstream from Seney: nothing is visible on either shore save the bushes extending out into the river from both banks.

10 min. in / 2 hr. 10 min. to go: The river floor is sandy and the water depth is at 2 feet. A creek merges at a severe angle from the left. Within 3 minutes, a large body of water (either a wide creek or a lagoon) is adjacent to the river's right. The Bear has a very rustic look. Gorgeous driftwood is everywhere.

15 min. in / 2 hr. 5 min. to go: Go left or right? A creek almost as wide as the river joins the water's flow from your left as the river bends right. Viewed from a distance, there's some question about which waterway is the main body of the river, i.e. should you follow the creek and paddle left or follow the river and paddle right? The answer comes when you arrive at this junction, where you see that the river current flows gently to the right.

2 minutes downstream, an attractive camp spot on dry, flat ground, well-shaded and with plenty of places to string up a hammock, is on the right shore as the river bends left.

20 min. in / 2 hrs to go: A creek merges at a severe angle from the left. One minute later, you paddle to a "T" in the river. As happened at the 15 minute mark, until you are just a few feet from this dual waterway junction, you do not know which way the main body of the river flows. At the junction, you'll follow the river current to the left. On the right is a lagoon that looks to run 100' deep into the marsh.

25 min. in / 1 hr. 55 to go: Excellent Frisbee break spot! As the river bends right, camping possibilities are seen on the left shore, where the forest floor is wide and flat. At the foot of this potential camp site, the river is 2' deep with a sandy, obstacle-free, bottom. A fine combination Frisbee and camp location.

35 min. in / 1 hr. 45 min. to go: At the end of a long straightaway, the river bends left and a fallen log completely blocks the river. Just right of midstream is where the log is closest to the waterline, and where you will be able to get out of your boat, balance yourself on the unmoving log while standing next to the boat, and push the canoe past the fallen log. On the long straightaway just downstream from this logjam, lies another fine Frisbee and break area: the water depth is 2', and the river floor is sandy and obstacle-free. This spot is marked by 2 nice-looking driftwood pieces near the right bank.

45 min. in / 1 hr. 35 min. to go: A creek, 7' wide at its mouth, extends deep into the woods, and joins the river from your left. Just beyond this creek, and along the right shore, is a beautiful piece of driftwood. Yellow wild irises begin to be seen near the left shore.

50 min. in / 1 hr. 30 min. to go: The Bear River "spreads" begins at the point where the river flows around a grassy island. The main body of the river is 30' wide and passes the island on the left. The right current is 15' wide. 2 minutes downstream, the river reconnects near the cattails. Two additional river splits and reconnects immediately follow. After this initial series of islands are passed, the river widens 150'. Lily pads, deer, and turtles are seen, as well as an outstanding Frisbee area with room for 20.

1 hr. 10 min. in / 1 hr. 10 min. to go: At the halfway point of the suggested trip, you are deep in the spreads. The river's main body flows right while a parallel current flows left with marsh land between the 2 waterways. Any number of little channels or canals may be ventured down and they'll all come back to the river. 2 minutes before the two big parallel waterways merge, had you paddled the left current you would be rewarded with the nicest looking campground today, with its flat and wide, high and dry, ground.

Kenny Sez: "That's handier than a pocket on a shirt."

1 hr. 18 min. in / 1 hr. 2 min. to go: Approach a big, grassy island populated with trees. Passing either right or left provides you with a current 25' wide. The downstream tip of the island is reached in 2 minutes. This signifies the end of the spreads.

1 hr. 23 min. in / 57 min. to go: You encounter evidence that a lumber mill operated nearby in the late-1800s. Near the right shore, visible 4' above the water surface, are the remains of a steam engine boiler explosion. Just downstream, you paddle over the sunken remains of a bridge, its pilings clearly seen.

1 hr. 27 min. in / 53 min. to go: Paddle through the first of 3 sets of culverts that are seen today. This first set of

culverts allows you to float beneath Evergreen Trail Road. The first two culvert sets are triple culverts, the last is a dual culvert.

1 hr. 40 min. in / 40 min. to go: Gorgeous driftwood piece lies parallel to the right bank. 70' downstream from the driftwood, steps lead up to a 7' tall diving platform on the left. Inexplicably, a simple canoeist begins singing Andy Williams "Moon River".

1 hr. 45 min. in / 35 min. to go: Foot path leads up to a possible camp spot, marked by fallen birch trees for the evening fire. Downstream one bend, on the left shore as the river bends right, a small deck sits immediately beneath the power lines.

1 hr. 52 min. in / 28 min. to go: At the top of the straightaway, twin cell phone towers come into view at the straightaway's end. Two minutes beyond is an A-frame with a unique wooden exterior chimney. Two minutes further downstream is a log cabin with a stone base. The river width tightens to 20' across and 5' deep.

2 hrs in / 20 min. to go: Traffic on the highway is 70' to your right. 3 minutes later, you float through the second set of culverts underneath Click Road.

2 hrs 6 min. in / 14 min. to go: Potential campground on the right shore as the river bends left, with plenty of birch on the site.

2 hrs 14 min. in / 6 min. to go: On the right shore is a white fence near the river's edge. A farm house is 200 yards in the distance.

2 hrs 17 min. in / 3 min. to go: Float through the final set of culverts, beneath McDougall Road.

2 hours and 20 minutes in: You are at the trip's end. Take out at the deck on the right.

THE TOWN: PETOSKEY

Detroit Tigers local radio affiliate: WMBN 1340 AM (Petoskey)

Arguably, the most beautiful stretch of highway in the state of Michigan begins 12 miles north of Petoskey, and ends at one of Michigan's oldest settlements, in the town of Cross Village. The 16 miles of M-119, running from north of Harbor Springs and ending at Cross Village, is also known as the "Tunnel of Trees". M-119 hugs the Lake Michigan shoreline and, for most of the drive, follows a high bluff that overlooks the Lake. The trees are grown close together near the edge of the road forming a canopy over the highway. This is a spectacular view when driving this road just before the sun sets to the west. The memories of your drive on M-119 will bring you a smile for years to come. If you take your drive in a sports car with the top down (a Spitfire comes to mind), the smile will be a bit bigger.

When your M-119 drive ends at Cross Village, you will want to stop and visit Legs Inn. Whether you dine indoors, where all of the tables and chairs are built from driftwood & tree stumps, or outdoors, on high ground with a gorgeous view of Lake Michigan, both ideas are good ones. Polish immigrant Stanley Smolak & his family built Legs Inn in the 1920s. The exterior and the interior are wonderful works of art and worth lingering over. The Legs Inn name relates to the row of inverted stove legs that make up the roof railing.

In the mid-1700s, the area stretching from Petoskey to Cross Village was referred to as "L'Arbre Croche", meaning "Crooked Tree". An estimated 18,000 Ottawa Indians made L'Arbre their home. In 1782, an Ottawa woman from Cross Village and a French fur trader became parents of one Ignatius Petoskey. Ignatius existed comfortably in both the world of the Europeans and the Native Americans, and he and his family accumulated much wealth and a great deal of land. Known also as "Chief Petoskey", he owned much of the land on which the city of Petoskey now stands. A national magazine reporter who visited the area in 1876 said that the old Chief was "the best-heeled Indian he had ever come across." Chief Ignatius Petoskey died in the town named for him in 1885.

The Village of Petoskey was incorporated in 1879, becoming a city in 1895. In addition to the area being a popular vacation destination, people from all over the country have come to the Petoskey area for relief during hayfever season. During the summer of 1882, the 1,200 residents of Petoskey hosted over 40,000 visitors! Taking advantage of this summer population spike, in 1902 The Petoskey Brewing Co. opened, with "Petoskey Sparkle" the brewery's most popular beer. The business operated under the agreement that the residents of Petoskey would vote every two years to determine if the brewery could remain open. The vote went their way the first 6 times, but vote number 7 was the brewery's unlucky number, and their doors closed in 1915.

Ernest Hemingway's childhood summers were spent in the Petoskey area, at the family cottage "Windemere" on Walloon Lake, the lake that is the source of Bear River. It was during these summer visits that Hemingway made friends with the local Odawa Indians and developed his respect for Indian culture. After serving as a World War I ambulance driver in Italy, he spent the winter of 1919 in Petoskey, and worked on his writing skills. Hemingway's "Nick Adams" stories are about the life and adventures of a boy in Northern Michigan.

The Nick Adams character shares the love for nature, fishing, and hunting that Ernest developed during his Michigan childhood summers.

Sources: "Up North Reflections" by the Petoskey News Review, www.legsinn.com, "The History of the Petoskey Area" by Harriet Kilborn, Little Traverse History Museum

THE TAVERN: DON'S BAR

Just before you turn off of US31 on to Division for the drive to the Bear River Canoe Livery, you'll see Don's Bar at 1041 N. US31, across from the Bay View Golf Course. Don's is a nothing fancy, shot and a beer bar. Sorry, no grill at Don's, only potato chips to go along with your post-canoeing beverage. Don, while no longer with us, bought the bar in 1962, and his wife's family owned the place before then. The tavern does feel 1960s with their old-time Stroh's and Carling Black Label wall décor, Pabst Blue Ribbon longnecks on hand (always a sure sign of quality), darts, pool table, and best of all, table top shuffleboard. But what Don's has an abundance of beyond anything else, is timeless wisdom via their wall signs…

- "Great Beer Bellies Are Made, Not Born"
- "We shoot every third salesman. The second one just left"
- "There are 3 kinds of people: those who make things happen, those who watch things happen, and those who wonder what happened"
- "In Poland they tell Michigan jokes"
- "If at first you don't succeed, quit. There's no sense being a damned fool about it"
- "A woman without a man is like a fish without a bicycle"

BETSIE RIVER
THOMPSONVILLE, MICHIGAN

RIVER SOUNDTRACK
Only Traces – Squeaky Clean
Cretins
When the Levee Breaks – Led
Zeppelin
Proud Mary – Ike & Tina Turner
Summertime Blues – Blue Cheer
The River of No Return – Tennessee
Ernie Ford

CANOE LIVERY
Betsie River Canoes & Campground
owner Mark McGee
13598 Lindy Road/Highway 602 (halfway between Crystal
Mountain Ski Resort & Thompsonville)
Thompsonville, Mi 49683. Ph (231) 879-3850
www.betsierivercanoesandcampground.com

RIVER QUOTE:
Maggie "When we hold our breath, we don't weigh as much." (her idea to avoid scraping the river bottom)

Betsie River

Level Two
Intermediate Ability Required

Detroit 241
Grand Rapids 138
Mackinaw City 133
Christmas, Mi. 261
Milwaukee, Wi. Birthplace of Pabst Blue Ribbon 396

THE BACKGROUND: BETSIE RIVER

There was excited anticipation for our float down a stretch of the Betsie River known as the "Upper Betsie". Depending on the source, we'd heard the Upper Betsie described as: (1) wild and scenic, with some sections requiring experience and (2) 7 miles of fast water. Both descriptions were attention grabbers.

Now, before we began our Upper Betsie adventure, old EMU friend Mark Kornheiser shared a Betsie story from his youth…

"My father owned land on the Betsie. In fact, there was a road that crossed a bridge over the Betsie that went right through his land. The road got bypassed by another road that went around it, and then his road over the bridge started getting little or no traffic. We would go up there in the summers and look around, and we started noticing that someone was stealing the bridge piece by piece. They started on the slats across the bridge, until they left only a few struts, maybe 2-3 feet wide, to walk across. Then they started stealing the bridge structure and the frame itself. Finally, someone from the Associated Press called us up one day and wrote a story about our stolen bridge. Maybe some concrete on both sides of the river would be all that is left."

17 minutes into today's trip, you'll pass this ghost bridge. It's marked by 10' high cement walls on opposite banks that, years ago, once supported a bridge that is now (say it Ernie) *"long… gone!"*

The Upper Betsie Culvert-Shooters: Tom Holbrook, Proud Mary Mitchell, Mag 'n me. Special thanks to livery man Bill, who provided great river details and pointed us to the tavern.

THE RIVER: PADDLING THE BETSIE

The suggested trip on the Upper Betsie is just under a 3 hour adventure. The put-in point is at the Wallin Road Bridge. Including the Wallin, you'll paddle under 5 bridges before taking out at bridge number 6, the Wolf Road Bridge (the site of the since removed Thompsonville Dam). There will be no authorized campgrounds, and the only toilets will be those at the Wolf Bridge take-out.

Put in 20' upstream from the Wallin Road Bridge. You will float through the Wallin's dual culverts, but before you do, please note that the culvert nearest the put-in river bank has a shallow ledge at its mouth. This ledge may grab your canoe and not want to let go. We suggest, when you first put-in, walking the canoes upstream and across the river to a point near the far shore. This will allow you to float through the far side culvert, where you'll enjoy a very fun ride through the tube.

Hold on tight for the first 15 minutes, 'cause the Upper Betsie has spunk! This river is very spirited right from the get go. You'll move quickly through many tight turns that get the paddling juices flowing. Very enjoyable.

On the 2nd bend past the culverts, there is a large rock midstream – be aware and avoid. In the early going, the river depth is 2', with a width of between 30' to 35'. There is a bit of bottom scraping going on.

8 min. in / 2 hrs 39 min. to go: Midstream sits a small island. The main current and the deeper water pass the island on the left. 2 minutes downstream, on the right bank, is an accessible-friendly dirt slope leading up to a picnic table. If you're ready to catch your breath after the first 10 minutes, pull on over for a break here.

14 min. in / 2 hrs 33 min. to go: "Betsie River Restoration Project" states the sign on the right bank. Almost $600,000 in state funding was very well-spent on the Betsie River to control erosion and improve the water quality. Just downstream is a little dirt slope on the right, another accessible-friendly pull-over point.

During the initial 15 minutes of today's trip, the current is fast with frequent runs of white water. The river tightens to as little as 10' from shore to shore, before widening back to 30'. The water depth is as little as 6" in some spots.

After the first 15 minutes, the river slows from its frenetic pace, settling into a nice, steady speed, remaining slightly faster than an average (as if there could be such a thing) Michigan River.

17 min. in / 2 hrs 30 min. to go: The 10' tall cement walls on opposite shores, a cement outcropping supporting nothing, & you're floating past the *"long… gone!"* ghost bridge. Whip-poor-wills are nocturnal creatures, but one that can't sleep keeps singing to us.

23 min. in / 2 hrs 24 min. to go: Pass both of the back-to-back islands on the right. The river is shallow enough so that you may bottom-out here and there.

49 min. in / 1 hr. 58 min. to go: At the big island, the little channel passing hard left is the most direct route, but may be clogged, while the main body of the river flows to the right. Pass the 2nd island on the left. Just downstream, the entire river is blocked except for an opening on the far right.

52 min. in / 1 hr. 55 min. to go: Dubbed by Maggie, "the homage to the gardener", showing just above the water's surface are 5 sets of pilings in groups of 4 running upstream to downstream. The top of each piling resembles green potted plants. This is a neat visual.

1 hour in / 1 hr. 47 min. to go: Float beneath the Long Road Bridge. 4 minutes downstream is a pretty sight on the left bank: 6 very small streams roll down the hillside, through the reeds, and on into the Betsie. We spot a blue heron.

1 hr. 8 min. in / 1 hr. 39 min. to go: You're below the Carmean Bridge. 6 minutes beyond is a sweet sight for all who aren't fond of mosquitoes: a colony numbering in the hundreds of skeeter-eatin' dragonflies sits in the shallows on the left. God bless each and every one of 'em!

1 hr. 17 min. in / 1 hr. 30 min. to go: At the end of a long straightaway, as the river bends right, is an island. Follow the main body of the river right to pass as the left is clogged.

4 minutes downstream, a deer 2' off of the right bank stands in the Betsie bent over for a sip of water. It sees us and bounds into the woods in an instant. Deer 1, camera zero.

Kenny Sez: "Aluminized: a rock just below the surface that's kissed many canoes"

1 hr. 27 min. in / 1 hr. 20 min. to go: Float past 30' high bluffs on both shores. A pair of bald eagles fly above us for the next few minutes.

1 hr. 41 min. in / 1 hr. 6 min. to go: At the end of a long straightaway is a large gray home as the river bends right. Mag begs to differ with my color description, claiming that the house is aubergine (I looked up the spelling). She soon decides the aubergine appearance is actually due to her tinted shades. All I know is that I learned a new word.

1 hr. 47 min. in / 1 hour to go: The fallen tree from the left blocks all but a 5' opening along the far right. Just beyond this are downed trees from each shore, and moments beyond that sits…

Frisbee heaven! Just before coming to the end of a short straightaway and a left river bend, the river has a beautiful, obstacle-free, sandy bottom. It is 40' across and 1' deep and a perfect Frisbee location.

2 hours in / 47 min. to go: Paddle through the culvert below the Thompsonville Bridge. 5 minutes downstream, as the river bends left, is a small island. Pass on the left, as we found the right to be too shallow. Thompsonville Road traffic is visible on your left.

2 hrs 14 min. in / 33 min. to go: A log fallen from the left bank is completely across the river, suspended above the water line. The most open space available to float under is just left of midstream. Based on our research, a chaise lounge chair, with its back in a straight and upright position, will barely scrape the bottom of the felled tree's bark as you glide beneath it.

2 hrs 18 min. in / 29 min. to go: King Road Bridge is reached – the last bridge before the Wolf Road Bridge exit. Clam shells are frequently seen on the river floor. The water is running 2' deep, and many logs are just below the surface, requiring your attention to avoid jarring or tipping the canoe.

2 hrs 38 min. in / 7 min. to go: The Little Betsie River merges from your left,

serving as the upstream border to a fine dirt & stone beach, also on the left.

The Little Betsie is the largest tributary of the Betsie, and is one-half its width, adding sufficient water volume to deepen the big Betsie noticeably. A fun little exercise is to stand in the water with one leg in the Betsie just upstream from the merger (nice cool water) and one leg in the Little Betsie (now that's a bit nippy!). Very refreshing.

At the small island seconds beyond the Big & Little confluence, the main body of the now suddenly chilled river flows left around the island.

2 hrs 44 min. in / 3 min. to go: *You hear it before you see it.* As the river bends right, you enjoy a brisk 1 minute white water run, flying down a straightaway and ending as the white water wraps around a bend. You pass between the concrete supports of a bridge no longer.

2 hours and 47 minutes, and you're in! Exit to the left on the dirt path at the base of the Wolf Road Bridge. As the top of the dirt path exit, a non-bottled Wild Turkey greets us.

At the parking lot, the nicely-maintained outhouse is a welcomed sight.

THE TOWN: FRANKFORT

Detroit Tigers local radio affiliate: WCCW 1310AM (Traverse City)

The town of Frankfort sits 20 miles to the northwest of Thompsonville. Had it not been for the sanctuary of the Betsie River, the town of Frankfort would not be called by that name… and, had it not been for a fierce Lake Michigan gale, the history of Frankfort would have been quite different. During the 1854 gale, Captain Snow looked up and down the Lake Michigan shoreline, seeking safety for his ship and his men. As he sought an opening among the thick lakeshore forest he saw the mouth of the Aux Bee Scies River ("Aux Bee Scies" is French for "the river of the Sawmill or Merganser Duck", spotted frequently while canoeing the Betsie. The name "Aux Bee Scies" eventually became the "Betsie" after being mispronounced by American Sailors). Captain Snow made his way past the shallow river mouth of the Aux Bee Scies, finding shelter in what is today known as Betsie Bay. Returning to his home port of Buffalo, Captain Snow spread the word about the outstanding natural harbor he'd found on the Lake Michigan shoreline. Snow was a native of Frankfurt, Germany. Besides being thankful for the refuge the area provided his ship and his men, he loved the area's natural beauty, and felt the port reminded him of his native Frankfurt. With a minor spelling modification, Captain Snow gave the city of Frankfort its name.

Frankfort's Point Betsie Lighthouse is easy on the eyes, and advertises itself as the 2nd most photographed lighthouse in the USA. Built in 1858, for years sailors used its beacon as their guide between the Manitou Islands and the Lake Michigan shoreline. Today, it's a very popular tourist attraction and serves as a key landmark during the annual Chicago to Mackinac Boat Race. Its automated modern light has a range of 15 miles, still lending navigation assistance to folks on the big lake over 150 years after it was first built.

Sources: Pat Kennedy, "Port City Perspectives" by Bixby & Sandman, "History of Alberta" by Black lock, www.shorelinevistorsguide.com, www.pointbetsie.org

THE TAVERN: LAUGHING HORSE SALOON - THOMPSONVILLE

On Highway 602, 2 miles straight east of the Betsie River Canoes & Campground and one-half mile east of downtown Thompsonville, the Laughing Horse Saloon looks like a big red barn. You can't miss it. Pabst Blue Ribbon – on tap!?! This relationship is off to a fine start. Even the Men's Room is marked with a very visible Pabst sign, to help guide you to the next step in the brewing process. Near the entrance are 2 hitching posts, in case you decide to ride Trigger or Traveller into the saloon for a visit. The room adjacent to the main bar has a big 'ole dance floor for some high stepping' fun. Let's see… 2 pool tables, a nice juke box, 3 video machines, and you can keep the kids busy (it's a costly diversion, though) at the claw machine. What's that behind the bar? A bumper sticker from Andy's Seney Bar (the bar at our beloved Fox River)! This tavern is alright by me.

BLACK RIVER ONAWAY, MICHIGAN

CANOE LIVERY:
Black River Canoe Outfitters / Ma & Pa's Country Store,
owners Darryl & Sharon Thivierge
M-33 & Hackett Lake Road (5 miles south of M-68),
Onaway, Mi 49765.
Phone (989) 733-8054
no website

RIVER QUOTE:
Tommy, "Doc, canoeing this river was one of your better ideas"

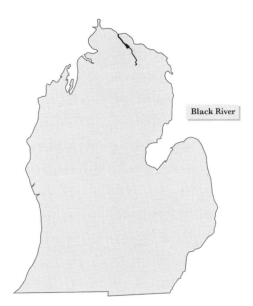

Black River

Level One
Beginner Ability Required

THE BACKGROUND: BLACK RIVER

The Black River has been designated as a "wild and scenic river". The Black River Gang of 3, Tom Holbrook, Kanoo Kenny Umphrey, and I, will second that emotion and say that the Black is a laid back, ain't no hurry, meander of a river. The Black River and its surroundings are peaceful and beautiful. Blue Herons, snapper turtles, and deer bounding from the river's edge were seen throughout our ride.

Michigan classifies the Black as a blue ribbon trout stream. Such designations are not given out lightly to either rivers or beers (see Pabst, 1893 World's Fair). To earn the blue ribbon classification, a river must be one of Michigan's best trout streams, support excellent stocks of wild resident trout, have the physical characteristics to permit fly casting, but be shallow enough to wade, have excellent water quality, and have earned a reputation for providing an excellent quality trout fishing experience. The Black is just the kind of river that might have enticed John Voelker to visit the Lower Peninsula.

THE RIVER: PADDLING THE BLACK

Suggested trip runs 2 hours and 15 minutes, putting in at Milligan Road, and taking out at 2 Mile, or Errat, Road. There are 2 major landmarks to help you determine your progress:

1)   Landmark #1 is an island seen at the 45 minute mark, one-third of the way into the float. The island is on your left, and you'll know that you're at the upstream tip of the island when you see what appears to be two large rivers merging. 4 minutes later, you're passing the downstream tip of the island when it again looks like to two large rivers are merging on your left. You now have 1 and one-half hours until the take out.

2)   Landmark #2 is a footbridge that you float beneath 1 hour and 45 minutes into the trip. Once at this bridge, there's 30 minutes remaining until the take out.

Along this 2 hour and 15 minute stretch of the Black River, there are no authorized campgrounds and no toilets.

4 min. in / 2 hrs 11 min. to go: The first obstacle is encountered quickly into today's ride in the form of a tree fallen from the left shore, while from the right branches lean into the river, leaving a 4' mid-stream gap to paddle through. 2 minutes later, and one

bend downstream from a creek merging from the right, a fallen tree and a tangle of debris are easily maneuvered around.

27 min. in / 1 hr. 48 min. to go: Back-to-back trees lean out into the river from the right shore. Around the next bend, 3 trees in succession lean in from the right bank, followed by a creek flowing into the river, also from your right.

31 min. in / 1 hr. 44 min. to go: A long creek, merging from the left, goes back deep into the woods.

35 min. in / 1 hr. 40 min. to go: From the right, a tangle of tree branches blocks two-thirds of the river. At its left end, a large tree trunk has been shorten by a power saw. At this same point in the river, from the left, a tree leans in. 70' further downstream a log lies mid-stream that can be easily passed on either side. The river depth here ranges from 2' to 4' with a width of 35'.

45 min. in / 1 hr. 30 min. to go: You've reached the first major landmark, the island on your left. From the left, at the island's tip, the waterway flowing into the river is very active, and is as large and as fast as the river itself. 2 minutes downstream, a birch tree leans into the river from the right shore, extending across two-thirds of the water.

49 min. in / 1 hr. 26 min. to go: The downstream tip of the island is reached.

51 min. in / 1 hr. 24 min. to go: Tree leaning in from the right shore covers 60% of the river. Fields of fern along the riverside begin to accompany us.

55 min. in / 1 hr. 20 min. to go: Tree fallen from the right bank blocks all but a 5' gap to paddle through along the left shore.

1 hr. in / 1 hr. 15 min. to go: On the left shore, 200 yards back from the river's edge, sits a house with a long, sloping lawn. Wooden chairs are along the shore.

Kenny Sez: "Where do books sleep? Between the covers"

1 hr. 6 min. in / 1 hr. 9 min. to go: At the end of a long straightaway as the river bends right, a nice looking log cabin with a green roof is near the shore. A brown cottage is next to it.

1 hr. 18 min. in / 57 min. to go: 3 consecutive fallen trees extend from the left bank as the river bends left. As you continue down a long straightaway, trees lean in from both river banks, all easily maneuvered around. A large gray house sits at the straightaway's end.

1 hr. 30 min. in / 45 min. to go: The dead creek on the right is the upstream border of a long, grassy expanse with 2 small homes.

1 hr. 37 min. in / 38 min. to go: In quick succession, a tree is fallen in from the right, a driftwood pile extends from the left, and a completely uprooted large tree from the right blocks one-half of the river.

1 hr. 39 min. in / 36 min. to go: A small northern version of Stone Mountain, a stone pile embedded into a hillside, is seen at the end of a long straightaway as the river flows left.

1 hr. 43 min. in / 32 min. to go: From a distance, the tree down from the left shore appears to completely block the river. As you float closer, you see that there is a 10' gap on the far right to paddle through as the river bends left.

1 hr. 45 min. in / 30 min. to go: You've reached major landmark #2 as you float beneath the foot bridge. Small rapids now begin as the river floor becomes rocky and the water depth shallows to 1' to 2'. For the balance of the trip, the entrancing calmness of the Black River is replaced by occasional runs of ripples or light rapids.

1 hr. 49 min. in / 26 min. to go: As the river bends left, a home sits on high ground with steps leading from the house to the river. The river here is 50' wide and 3' deep.

1 hr. 52 min. in / 23 min. to go: The yellow "frog crossing" sign is on the left riverbank. Beyond here, as the river bends right, is a light rapids run as the river shallows to 1' deep.

2 hr. 2 min. in / 13 min. to go: As the river bends left, a long and choppy rapids run lasts the entire length of the straightaway. The waves put a bounce under your boat.

2 hr. 12 min. in / 3 min. to go: A beautiful large A frame with many windows is seen ahead on the right.

2 hours and 15 minutes in: You reach the take out point. Exit right at the stairs just before the 2 Mile (or Errat) Road Bridge.

THE TOWN: ONAWAY

Detroit Tigers local radio affiliate: WIDG 940 AM (Cheboygan)

Onaway is located at the junction of M-68 and M-33, 45 miles to the southeast of the Straits of Mackinac. The town was settled in the 1880s as a logging community. In 1886 it was given the name "Onaiweh", an Ojibwa Indian cry meaning "awake", referenced in Henry Wadsworth Longfellow's poem, "Hiawatha". The poem spoke romantically of northern Michigan and Wisconsin Indian lore.

Onaway is located on the western edge of beautiful Presque Isle County. For a time during Prohibition years, Presque Isle County was dry and neighboring Cheboygan County was wet. This situation made the road between Onaway and Tower (a town located on the eastern edge of Cheboygan County) as busy as a big-city rush hour.

"Onaway Steers The World" was the well-earned slogan for the Lobdell-Emory Plant, the 1920s manufacturing site of wooden steering wheels for the American automobile industry. No plant anywhere in the world produced more wooden steering wheels, or wooden bicycle rims, than the 44 acre Onaway plant. Tiny Onaway continued to be the world leader in steering wheel production until a January 1926 fire destroyed the plant, and almost the town itself. The story, as told in news accounts…

"One crisp morning in January 1926, the fire whistle blew and as is the custom, everyone rushed to the door and window to find out where the fire was. In the west they saw huge clouds of black smoke rising from the Lobdell and Bailey mills. Stores, homes, offices were abandoned, and every citizen went to the fire. By nightfall, Onaway's backbone was broken. By the end of the week, thousands of laborers left the city to seek employment elsewhere."

Homes were abandoned and taken over by squatters. Merchants closed their stores. The city was left with a heavy debt as most of the taxpayers had left town. The few who remained were a determined lot who successfully worked to reduced Onaway's expenditures and indebtedness and started the town on a comeback. In the 1980s, the Michigan State Legislature designated Onaway the "Sturgeon Capital of Michigan." The Sturgeon is a prehistoric fish that can live as long as 150 years old, with an average weight of 60 pounds (the biggest on record ever caught was 193 pounds), and has an average length of 3 to 4 feet (with some in excess of 6' long). This fish is found in the deepest waters of Black Lake, with an average of 16 caught annually.

10 miles to the east of town on M-68 are the Ocqueoc (pronounced *ack-e-ack*) Falls, the largest waterfall in the Lower Peninsula. After visiting various Upper Peninsula falls, the first thought is that these are small and, relative to the U.P. falls, the Ocqueoc Falls are. However, you soon find yourself entranced in watching the Ocqueoc River with graceful speed flow down gorgeously over each step of the Falls. The memory is worth your time.

Sources: "Onaway Awakens", www.onawaychamber.com

THE TAVERN: NORTHLAND BAR

Less than a 10 minute drive from the Black River Canoe Outfitters, on M-68 in the town of Onaway, you can unwind after a canoeing adventure at the Northland Bar. Dave Havel is the owner of the Northland, and is a very pleasant sort. Dave did a fine job in hiring bar help, as waitress Jill took good care of our table while conversing fluently with us in canoe-talk. The Northland bar burgers did the trick, and Pabst Blue Ribbon (a sure sign of quality) is on hand to round out the meal. Evidently, the town folk's taste is not that demanding, as Jill said this was the first time in all of her years that she had ever served an entire table of patrons PBRs. The Northland has 4 pool tables (no waiting), 2 video games, an old time piano, and a juke box to round out a relaxing visit.

CASS RIVER
VASSAR, MICHIGAN

CANOE LIVERY:
Cork Pine Canoe Rental
owners Susan & Gary Matthews
132 S. Water St, Vassar MI 48768.
Phone (989) 863-0103
www.corkpinecanoerental.com.

RIVER QUOTE:
Lurch, "Neat. Sweet. Petite."

RIVER SOUNDTRACK:
Step Right Up – Tom Waits
Who Drank My Beer (While I Was In The Rear)? – Buster Poindexter
Saginaw Michigan – Lefty Frizzell
No Regrets – Von Bondies,
Rollin' & Tumblin' Part 1 – Baby Face Leroy Trio

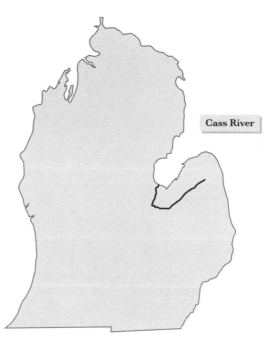

Cass River

Level One
Beginner Ability Required

THE BACKGROUND: CASS RIVER

"Let's go to the Thumb!" Now what Michigan native can resist that clarion call? The very thought of the Thumb conjures up visions of small towns, rolling farmlands, lighthouses, wind turbines (32 in the town of Pigeon alone), and sparkling sunshine glistening off of the waters of Lake Huron (sunrise), Saginaw Bay (sunset), and countless inland waterways.

90 minutes north of Metro Detroit, and 7 miles to the northeast of historic ("taste like chicken") Frankenmuth, sits the town of Vassar and the Cork Pine Canoe Rental, our gateway to the Cass River. The road from Frankenmuth to Vassar runs alongside the Cass, parallel to and just north of the river.

Including its north and south branches, the Cass River runs for a very leisurely 120 miles. It flows into the Shiawassee River in the Shiawassee National Wildlife Refuge, just before the Shiawassee merges with the Tittabawassee River, southwest of Saginaw. *Side note*: a great way to see the Shiawassee Wildlife Refuge, "Michigan's Everglades", is on a modified flat bottom boat with the folks at "Johnny Panther Quests".

The Cass River is beautiful, but shallow beyond mid-summer. Our Cass trip was taken the first week of September. At this time of the year, unless there's been a recent rainfall, you should float the Cass in a kayak: our canoes bottomed out several times, requiring at least one person in the canoe to get out and push the canoe through the low water.

The Cass River Bottom-Scrapers: Doubles & Ken Verba, Scott Halloran, Janet, Alex & Austin Quick-Finch, Justin Brown, Jerry (Crawdaddy) Japes, Lisa, Dan, Taylor, Renee, Jamie & Tim Dempsey, Julie, Colonel, Eric, Karen & Big Joe Braun, Maggie & Doc.

THE RIVER: PADDLING THE CASS

The suggested trip runs 3 hours and 30 minutes. The put in is at the M46 Bridge, just northeast of Vassar. You'll paddle below 3 additional bridges before the take out point.

The Kane Road Bridge is 1 hour and 10 minutes downstream from the M46 Bridge. The train trestle and M15 Bridge are both within 10 minutes of the trip's end. The take out is 5 minutes downstream from the M15 Bridge, just a few feet before the ruins of a dam. There are no campgrounds and no toilets on the suggested trip.

River notes: keep in mind that our expedition was taken the first week in September, late in the season. The river ran very shallow, much more than you would encounter in the Spring through mid-Summer. The low water affects the trip from the start: just past the M15 Bridge is a 100-yard walk through, the first of eleven experienced today. Rocks are found throughout, from palm-sized to big rocks measuring an estimated 15' in diameter.

Cork Pine Canoe Rental includes wooden paddles with their canoes – a great touch! Cork Pine rents wide-bottom fiberglass boats with built-in holders for fishing poles & drinking cups. Maggie adds that these canoes are very lounge chair friendly.

20 min. in / 3 hr. 10 min. to go: The river runs 50' wide and 4" – 6" deep, with a great deal of bottom-scraping. This 6-mile journey is a slow and pleasant meander.

25 min. in / 3 hr. 5 min. to go: First creek you'll see today merges from the right at a severe diagonal. 3 minutes downstream, a ledge on the right precedes a 120' long stretch of light rapids. You'll veer left around this ledge and then immediately cut back right: through this 120' light rapids run, the river is too shallow to float left or center.

**Kenny Sez: "The lumber store fella asked me how long I'd need the 2" by 4"s.
I told him, pretty long – we're using 'em to build a garage"**

30 min. in / 3 hr. to go: a very small creek with a very loud voice merges from the right.

Within the first 50 minutes of the float, Tim has reeled in a smallmouth bass, a rock bass, and a pike. However, accidents happen to even the best fishermen & paddlers, and we're soon reminded why you should always include a first aid kit with your river gear. One of Tim's fishing hook barbs caught in his wrist (it sounds as bad as it looked). The wound was cleaned up nicely with antiseptic and wound wipes. Much to the chagrin of the fish, Tim was casting lines again just a few moments later.

1 hr. 10 min. in / 2 hr. 20 min. to go: Float beneath the Kane Road Bridge. 5 minutes downstream, look to the left bank: an old-time windmill sits 150' beyond the shoreline. The river soon deepens to 2'.

1 hr. 50 min. in / 1 hr. 40 min. to go: Midstream sits a giant climbing rock, 7' in diameter and, during this shallow September season, extending 3' above the water's surface.

2 hr. 45 min. in / 45 min. to go: If it hasn't already been called it, it should be. "The Rock of Vassar", a 15' in diameter rock, lies along the left shore.

3 hr. 20 min. in / 10 min. to go: Paddle below the train trestle. 5 minutes downstream, you float beneath the M15/Main Street Bridge.

3 hours 30 minutes: The trip ends. Exit on the left shore, a few feet before the ruins of a dam (destroyed in the 70s).

THE TOWN: VASSAR

Detroit Tigers local radio affiliate: WSGW 790 AM (Saginaw)

Lewis Cass was Michigan's Territorial Governor from 1813 to 1831. While on a visit to Chippewa Indian tribes in the area, Cass couldn't help but notice the impressive forests of timber, and soon encouraged the investors and the lumbermen to come. In the 1830s, the river was named after him.

In 1849, Townsend North and James M. Edmunds liked what they saw in the area. Along the banks of the Cass River, they built a settlement and commissioned the building of a dam. The town that they started was named after Edmund's uncle, Matthew Vassar, who later founded Vassar College in New York.

Vassar is known as the "Cork Pine City". It is located at the midpoint between the towns of Caro & Bridgeport. In the mid-1800s, between these 2 towns, were 5 natural driftwood dams. Once the lumbermen had these dams removed, allowing cut logs to be floated to mills downstream, Vassar's position as a major lumber town was established. The type of white pine that grew in dense forests along the Cass River in Vassar was cork pine. Cork pine trees grew to heights of 150' and diameters up to 4'. The fact that cork pine was strong, lightweight, and had unusual buoyancy (it floated "like a cork") made it the variety of white pine in greatest demand. One of the biggest markets for the cork pine was for homes and buildings as our country's western territories were being settled.

The Flood of 1986 was known simply as "the Flood" to those affected. This covered a 60 mile wide band across central Lower Michigan. Vassar was among the unfortunate locales that received the heaviest rainfall at 14", most of which fell on 9-11 (hmm). The heavy rains combined with the opening of the Caro dam, forcing water well over the river banks. In downtown Vassar, folks were traveling down Main Street in rowboats. Water was 8' up the wall at the movie house, and within 2' of the ceiling at the Hardware Store.

Sources: Susan Matthews, Michigan Historical Marker in Vassar, patrons in Betty Lou's Restaurant, www.trnews.com

THE TAVERN: VASSAR BAR

The sign out front just says "Liquor Bar", but the folks that we talked to all called it the Vassar Bar. Since Wayne's Bar burned down a couple of years back, the Vassar Bar has been the only game in town. The tavern sits downtown on Main Street, near Huron Street, about one half-mile from the Cork Pine Canoe Rental. The Vassar Bar patrons are a determined lot, making their way to the pub by rowboat during the flood of '86. After the flood, everything in Vassar dried out, 'cept the folks in here.

This bar has an old time feel. We had a smiling flashback, courtesy of the bar's pull-lever cigarette machine. There's no Pabst Blue Ribbon offered, but the Vassar Bar does have Stroh's to quench your thirst. While you're sipping your Stroh's, you can listen to some tunes on the bar's juke box or shoot a game or two of pool. There's a big ole dance floor in the adjacent room, closed off from the rest of the pub 'til the Friday night live music starts up. Last but not least, the Vassar Bar's burgers received multiple "two thumbs up!" from our Cass River Bottom- Scrapers.

CRYSTAL RIVER
GLEN ARBOR, MICHIGAN

RIVER SOUNDTRACK:
On The Road Again – Willie Nelson
Pipeline – George Bedard & the Kingpins
Crystal Blue Persuasion – Tommy James
& the Shondells
Down To The River To Pray – Alison
Krauss
Please Don't Bury Me – John Prine

CANOE LIVERY
Crystal River Outfitters
owners Katy & Matt Wiesen
6249 W. River Rd.
Glen Arbor MI 49696
Phone (231) 334-4420
www.crystalriveroutfitters.com.

RIVER QUOTE: Overheard at our launch point…
"Dad, how many mosquito bites before we run out of blood?"

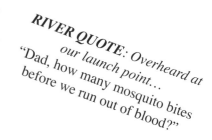

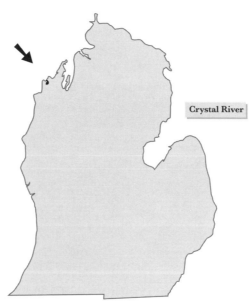

Crystal River

Level One
Beginner Ability Required

THE BACKGROUND: CRYSTAL RIVER

The Crystal River earns its name: the crystal clear water allows you to easily see the river floor while floating downstream. In addition to the great water clarity, this river has a beautiful, rustic, look and feel about it. There are two portages to contend with (nothing too bad) and one culvert to shoot through (very fun). Be aware that if you wish to enjoy the Crystal in a canoe, it is suggested that you take the trip before the end of June, or after a rain storm raises the water level. Once June has passed, the Crystal River might best be appreciated in a kayak. Canoeing in early-July, the shallow river bottom forced us into a half-dozen walk-throughs, the final two accompanied by language normally reserved for a blown 9th inning lead by old Tiger closers Todd Jones, Mike Henneman, or Aurelio "Senor Smoke" Lopez. God bless 'em all.

Research team member Tommy was told that the river was so low in 2007, much of it was not navigable. The story goes that the dam at the launch point controls the water level for both Crystal Lake and the Crystal River. Control of the dam is in the hands of the Crystal Lake Association, who made decisions on water control that contributed to the 2007 difficulties. An agreement has since been reached that the river must stay at certain minimal levels to allow canoeing or, at least, kayaking.

Make a note to bring whatever bug protection works for you: two young ladies paddled up to us at the second portage, and one of the ladies (who had applied no protection) had at least 20 large, swollen, mosquito bites on her back. With a minimum application of Deet (which we loaned to the swollen paddler after the horse was already out the barn door), we had minimal bug problems.

The Crystal Blue Persuaders & Research Team: Mary Mitchell, Tommy Holbrook, Maggie, and Doc.

THE RIVER: PADDLING THE CRYSTAL

The suggested trip runs 2 hours and 25 minutes, with most of it flowing through the Sleeping Bear Dunes National Lakeshore. The 7 mile float starts at Fisher Road, putting in 2 to 3 minutes upstream from the previously-mentioned dam, and is marked by a sign that announces, "Portage & Dam .3 mi ahead". As you begin, the river is 1' deep, 50' wide, and its floor is covered with sand, seaweed, clam shells, and stones. When you reach the dam, portage to the right, a 20' walk.

Early into your river journey, the large quantity of trees that have fallen into the water presents an enjoyable challenge to your paddling skills. The slow current provides you with plenty of time to line your canoe up to easily float through the unblocked sections of the Crystal.

10 minutes into the trip, trees lean over from each bank at a 45 degree angle, the tips of each touching each other, forming a beautiful canopy over your boat. There is a great deal of bottom-skimming.

37 min. in / 1 hr. 48 min. to go: As the river bends left, a small island approximately 20' long – populated by a single tree – is too tempting to pass up as a break spot. Based on the number of cherry seeds left behind by our Crystal Blue Persuaders, that single tree may have some company in the not too distant future. Many kayakers float by us during our break (our first clue that perhaps that's the best mode of transport this late into the season), as well as multiple schools of small fish.

Seconds downstream from the island, and merging from your right, is a dead creek 30' wide at its mouth and impressively clogged with fallen trees and tangles of branches.

Beginning with this river-creek junction, the river becomes very shallow, requiring the members of one of our research canoes to twice get out of their canoe for a few seconds, relieving the boat's weight and allowing it to continue to float downstream.

Also at this point is a gorgeous visual: looking down the long straightaway, every few feet trees from opposite riverbanks seem to be taking turns falling into the river, first one from the left, then one from the right, then again from the left, and so on. There is plenty of room to paddle around each of these obstructions.

45 min. in / 1 hr. 40 min. to go: "River bank restoration" says the sign on the left shore. The thin strip of land that the sign sits on barely separates you from a section of the river one bend downstream, and going in the opposite direction, of your canoe. A slight stretch of your neck will allow you to look past the sign and see the downstream river flow. You will know that the restoration sign is 2 minutes downstream when you pass the creek merging at a severe angle from the right.

Trees leaning in from opposite banks meet in midstream well above your head. Where the trees meet, the tree tips come to a point, giving one (or at least me) the impression of weapons to be used in an upcoming swordfight by teams of giants. Or could they be toothpicks for very large bears?

1 hr. in / 1 hr. 25 min. to go: With the triple culverts (also known as tubes) in sight at the end of a straightaway, the right shore offers up a 200' long stretch of flat ground that would make a fine campsite. Please note: any campsite mentioned in today's trip is neither an authorized nor a maintained site.

Float quickly through the culvert – great fun! Take the far left culvert (offering the most space for your boat) and lean back for the fast, short, downhill thrill run. This is like the quick burst of an amusement park ride. Once past the culverts, the river turns hard left. If you cannot make the turn, no problem. You'll simply bump into the rocks along the right shore, straighten yourself out, and continue on the journey.

Note: If the water level is too high to run the culverts, portage to your left just upstream. Walk your canoes a few feet to the left and ahead of you to where the friendly ground slopes back to the river.

10 minutes downstream from the culverts, the river deepens to 2' and the riverbanks take on a much different look: the fallen or leaning trees seen so frequently are replaced by 2' tall reeds, irises, and meadows along both shores.

1 hr. 20 min. in / 1 hr. 5 min. to go: On the right bank, the flat ground runs along a 300' stretch of the straightaway. If you can get past the 15' wide swath of reeds protecting the shore, this makes for a fine break spot. At the straightaway's end sits an island of reeds. Passage on the right is wide open, while the left is a bit clogged (and may make a good adventure).

1 hr. 25 min. in / 1 hr. to go: 70' long school of driftwood lies in shallow water on the right.
3 minutes downstream, a 400' long straightaway, complete with a 1' deep and obstacle- free sandy bottom, is almost the best Frisbee break spot that the Crystal has to offer. I say "almost" for 2 reasons: (1) there are fallen logs along each riverbank and (2) I've seen what the river looks like 3 minutes downstream.

3 minutes downstream, just past 5 bat houses on the left shore, is a long straightaway where the river is 6" deep, with a sandy & obstacle-free floor: the finest Frisbee break spot on the Crystal. The area is marked by 3 homes along the right shore with some mighty good looking decks.

Kenny Sez: *"Changes in Latitudes, Changes in Attitudes. It works in Michigan like it does in the Carribean"*

1 hr. 38 min. in / 47 min. to go: On a tight left bend, the ground slopes nicely from the right bank. As you approach the island just downstream, stay to the right. There are lily pads everywhere. Sadly, so are sections of the river so shallow that walk-throughs are needed.

1 hr. 45 min. in / 40 min. to go: A 70' sandy island, along the right side of the river, is a great break spot!

1 hr. 55 min. in / 30 min. to go: As the river bends right, you encounter a very long island passable either left or right (with the right the clearer path).

2 hrs in / 25 min. to go: Encounter today's second set of triple culverts, with openings much too small for canoers or kayakers, but just about right for those water-skiing squirrels (I've always admired those little fellers, especially when they ski with one leg up in the air). This will require the final Crystal River portage. Exit the river on your right, at the beautiful stone tribute: "Dave Marks Portage – He Carried This River In His Heart". Cross the road after looking both ways (675 County Road can be very busy), and re-enter the river on the right bank.

During the final 25 minutes of the float, there are multiple submerged pilings that you need to be aware of. These are just below the surface, and colliding with one might pose problems to keeping your canoe upright.

2 hrs 12 min. in / 13 min. to go: Approach back-to-back islands, both to be passed on the left (right passage is completely clogged).

2 hrs 15 min. in / 10 min. to go: Viewed from upstream, it appears that the entire river is blocked by debris. Approach and pass this slowly. You first pass a tangle of brush from the right shore. 10' beyond, a tree fallen from the left blocks 75% of the river.

2 hours and 25 minutes: you've arrived at the livery and your Crystal River adventure is concluded. Exit the river on the left.

THE TOWN: GLEN ARBOR & THE SLEEPING BEAR NATIONAL LAKESHORE

Detroit Tigers local radio affiliate: WCCW 1310 AM (Traverse City)

The town of Glen Arbor sits on a sandbar formed between Lake Michigan and Glen Lake. It is located within the 71,000 acre Sleeping Bear Dunes National Lakeshore at the southwest corner of the Leelanau Peninsula. Should your maps be missing or your GPS be out of order, the intoxicating aroma emitting from the Leelanau Coffee Roasting Company will lead you to this very charming village.

Dominating the Leelanau western shoreline, and found just south of Glen Arbor, is Sleeping Bear Dunes National Lakeshore. Pulitzer-prize winning author, and Benzie County's favorite son, Bruce Catton described the ever-shifting dunes this way, *"Two miles high, hundreds of miles wide, and many centuries deep"*. The Dunes are a masterpiece sculpted by nature, and the labor done by wind, water, and ice is a work in progress. Noticeable geological changes normally evolve over thousands, if not millions, of years. The Dunes are an exception to this: over the last 100 years alone, landslides at Sleeping Bear Point have twice resulted in large sections of land plunging into Lake Michigan. At times, shifting sands bury trees and then, when the dunes move on, "ghost forests" of previously buried dead trees are exposed.

The massive shoreline dunes feature bluffs as high as 460 feet above Lake Michigan Note: Although the public may descend the very steep 460' bluff to the edge of Lake Michigan, keep in mind you then have to ascend the same bluff if you'd like to get back home. Top of the bluff sign warning that the climb is "extremely exhausting" should be taken into consideration.

"Sleeping Bear really stands out from space. There is a sharp contrast between the white of the dunes, and the vast aqua of Lake Michigan, the deep blue of Glen Lake and the green of the forests." U.S. astronaut and Michigan native Jack Lousma

Archaeologists assert that, beginning in 500 A.D. and continuing for over a 1,000 year period, a Benzie County riverbank was a favorite Indian gathering spot for large gatherings or celebrations. That's longer than many of Sam Kinison's parties. The Chippewa Indian legend regarding how the Sleeping Bear Dune & the Manitou Islands were created is...

"Long ago, in the land that is now Wisconsin, a mother bear and her two cubs were driven into Lake Michigan by a raging forest fire. They swam and swam, but soon the cubs tired and lagged far behind. Mother bear finally reached the opposite shore and climbed to the top of a bluff to watch and wait for her cubs. Too tired to continue, the cubs drowned within sight of the shore. The Great Spirit Manitou created two islands to mark the spot where the cubs disappeared and then created a solitary dune to represent the faithful mother bear."

When the Chippewa Indians gave Sleeping Bear Dunes its name, they gave what is today known as Glen Lake the name of Bear Lake. European settlers later changed the name to Glen Lake.

Sources: *Footprints Where Once They Walked* by Nan Helm, www.leelanau.com, *Sleeping Bear: Its Lore, Legends, and First People* by George Weeks, *The Road Guide: Sleeping Bear Dunes National Lakeshore* by Susan Stites, U.S. Department of the Interior

THE TAVERN: ART'S TAVERN

Glen Arbor's Art's Tavern is conveniently located just a few feet away from the Crystal River Outfitters. The sign at Art's door invites you to "please wait to be seated or belly up to the bar", an invitation that we could hardly refuse. This bar has personality, as does its wait staff. We were taken care of by Dave Dilley (*dill-e*, please), who did an expert job entertaining us with the historical and current fun facts of the pub, while simultaneously filling in a timely fashion our Pabst (always a sure sign of quality) longnecks orders and food orders (excellent burgers!).

Listed on the menu under a section entitled "Beers your Grandfather used to drink" is not only Pabst Blue Ribbon, but also Strohs, Blatz, and ("Hey Mabel!") Black Label. Both of my Grandfather's would have liked Art's.

Art's pool table is tucked beneath the floor during the daytime hours, creating room for 2 more tables of art-lovers to be seated at chow time. In the evening, the pool table is hydraulically raised for night time entertainment. Now that's pretty cool.

The ceiling is almost completely covered with pennants from colleges, high schools, & pro sports teams. To no one's surprise, the pennant from Eastern Michigan University stands out the most: it's the dirtiest, representative of the blue-collar grit that EMU exudes. At least it does in the mind of a Huron.

The most fascinating objects hanging from the ceiling are not pennants, though. They are two skis, one a snow ski and one a water ski. And, although they are suspended from the ceiling of a tavern, these are working skis. Attached to each of the two skis are 5 coolies (i.e. beer can insulators). At unannounced moments, the skis are brought down from the ceiling, and shots placed in each of the 5 coolies. 5 bar patrons hold up one ski, each patron positioned in front of one coolie. The ski is lifted to head level, tipped sideways, and the shots consumed. First time for everything, mm, my ears still ring. It should be mentioned here that these skis are referred to as "shot-skis". I really do like this place!

DOWAGIAC RIVER
DOWAGIAC, MICHIGAN

RIVER SOUNDTRACK:
All Summer Long – Kid Rock
Impromptus No. 4 (Fantaisie-Impromptu)
– Frederic Chopin
Yes, The River Knows – Doors
Straighten Up & Fly Right – Nat King Cole
Hold It Right There – Big Dave and the
Ultrasonics

CANOE LIVERY
Doe-Wah-Jack's Canoe Rental
owner Randy Rea
52963 M51 N (4 mi north of Dowagiac)
Dowagiac MI 49047
(269) 782-7410
www.paddledcri.com.

RIVER QUOTE:
Ronnie Junior, 8 years old, upon
hearing warnings of river obstacles
ahead, "We'll take the risk of turning
upside down."

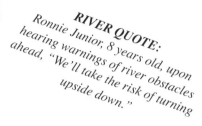

Dowagiac River

Level Two
Intermediate Ability Required

THE BACKGROUND: DOWAGIAC RIVER

Floating down the Dowagiac River was one of the finest surprises that we experienced while researching this book. The river feel was rustic (even more than most rivers), the water flowed quickly down long straight-aways, the many logs just above and just below the surface kept us alert and on our toes, and the trees leaning in from each bank formed a canopy above us the duration of the ride, acting as a coolant on a hot summer day.

The long straight-aways are the result of a 1920s decision to channelize the river, in order to facilitate drainage for agricultural purposes. This turned 20 miles of a slow moving, meandering waterway into 15 miles of a fast moving ditch.

There is a popularly-support move afoot to restore the original, meandering flow, of the Dowagiac, led by a group called "Partnership for MEANDRS" (Meeting Ecological and Agricultural Needs within the Dowagiac River System). The group looks to reverse the effects of the high speed of the straight-aways, which contributes to erosion, degrades the water quality, and limits habitant diversity. The thinking is that, with 90% of the river's flow coming from the groundwater, making it one of the largest coldwater streams in southwest Michigan, restoration of the river meanders would allow the Dowagiac to become a blue ribbon trout stream, rivaling northern Michigan Trout Rivers such as the Upper Manistee and the Au Sable.

As of the end of 2008, a one quarter mile stretch of the Dowagiac, running through Dodd Park, has had its original flow restored. The results have been well-received, and MEANDRS is eager to restore other sites along the river. As most of the river flows through privately owned land, obtaining approvals to reconnect any long stretches of the meanders may be a difficult task, although one landowner has expressed interest in restoring a 3/4 mile meander on his property.

Our ride down the Dowagiac River in its current, fast flowing, straight-away form was a very enjoyable one for each of us. Although floating the river with its meanders restored may also be a happy adventure, to experience the river in its unique current shape, we suggest that the Dowagiac River be added to your canoeing and kayaking list very soon.

Sources: DNR website, Randy Rea, Barbara Cook of MEANDRS

The Dowagiac Ditch crack researchers: Ron Swiecki & Ronnie Jr., Tommy Holbrook, Theresa Melching, Bret Holbrook, Kanoo Kenny Umphrey, his grandson Ethan Chandler Blake, and me.

THE RIVER: PADDLING THE DOWAGIAC

The suggested trip ran our group exactly 2 hours. We launched at the river's edge in front of the Doe-Wah-Jack livery, and took out at the M62 Bridge. Four vehicle bridges will be seen on this trip: the M51 Bridge (100' downstream from the livery), Middle Crossing Bridge (the half-way point), the Yaw Street Bridge (30 minutes from the end) and M62. Livery man Neal knows the river well and passed long very helpful information to us.

As we put in, the river is 25' wide and 2' deep. Almost immediately after floating past the M51 Bridge, we have a river traffic jam as we work our way around a big tangle of brush on the water. Stay to the left.

This river is a joy to paddle! The long straight-aways are a kick to float, the water is moving at a good clip, the river is tight shore-to-shore, and the natural tree canopy above us is a thing of beauty. 13 minutes downstream from our launch, separated by 100 yards, two trees fallen from one side of the river to the other lie well above us on the high banks, so no limbo is required. The banks are high the entire 2 hour trip.

15 min. in / 1 hr. 45 min. to go: We float beneath the first of two footbridges seen today. 7 minutes downstream, we once again float well-below two fallen trees, these separated by 80', and lying above us on the high banks.

No boredom today! Tangles of cut trees are everywhere throughout the river, challenging us as we maneuver through and around each obstacle. It was at this point, responding to the warning shouts of what lies ahead, that 8-year old Ronnie Jr. announced that he and his Dad would "take the risk of turning upside down". Ron Sr. mentions that if he brings the kid home dead, he'll have to deal with the wife.

Did we say "rustic"? The forest hugs the river's edge with its dark beauty. We have our third muskrat sighting. Brook trout and chubs are floating past us.

30 min. in / 1 hr. 30 min. to go: From the right, a very spirited, but clogged, creek flows towards the river with energy. 5 minutes downstream, is our first view of the many, long thin creeks that we'll see today.

37 min. in / 1 hr. 23 min. to go: Here's the first fallen tree that requires us to limbo beneath it. It's fallen from the right, and may be passed anywhere from midstream to the far left.

40 min. in / 1 hr. 20 min. to go: Paddle below the 2nd of two footbridges on this trip.

47 min. in / 1 hr. 13 min. to go: Hey good lookin'! A fine, strong-flowing creek merges from your right.

55 min. in / 1 hr. 5 min. to go: Pass below another shore-to-shore, high banks, non-limbo fallen tree. Approaching from a distance, it appears to be a footbridge.

Kenny Sez: "The logs that you don't see are more dangerous than the ones you do."

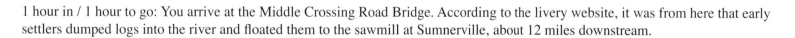

1 hour in / 1 hour to go: You arrive at the Middle Crossing Road Bridge. According to the livery website, it was from here that early settlers dumped logs into the river and floated them to the sawmill at Sumnerville, about 12 miles downstream.

1 hr. 30 min. in / 30 min. to go: You reach the Yaw Street Bridge. There will be one-half hour remaining in the trip.

2 hours in, and the M62 Bridge take-out is on the right. Upon stepping on to dry land, Ronnie Junior asks, "So, where's the bar?" The kid understands that the book research work must continue.

THE TOWN: DOWAGIAC

Detroit Tigers local radio affiliate: WSJM 1400 AM (St. Joe / Benton Harbor).

Dowagiac is located in the southwest corner of Michigan, 30 minutes north of the Indiana State Line, and midway between Kalamazoo and South Bend, Indiana. It is a part of Cass County, named after Lewis Cass, Governor of the Michigan Territory from 1813 to 1831. The town and the county were part of a glacial lake, 120 miles long and 10 miles wide, that stretched from Grand Rapids in the north to South Bend in the south.

The name Dowagiac derives from the Potawatomi Indian word "Ndowagayuk" which means (depending on your research source) either "foraging ground" or "fishing water". Either definition of the Indian word would be appropriate for an area richly blessed with fish, wild game, grains, fruit, vegetables, and medicinal herbs. In 1824, as the first white settlers arrived, the area was inhabited primarily by the Potawatomi tribe. The influx of Europeans jumped in 1836, when the stagecoach route linking Kalamazoo and Niles (then known as Carey Mission), and running through Dowagiac, was established. The stagecoach route followed the old Grand River Indian trail.

The Doe-Wah-Jack's Canoe Rental is named after a fictional Native American Indian, Chief Doe-Wah-Jack. The chief's creation occurred during the early days of telephones: when speaking with telephone operators, customers had trouble pronouncing the name "Dowagiac", so the chief's name was born as a phonetic way to remedy the problem.

P.D. Beckwith and the Round Oak Stove were to Dowagiac what Henry Ford and the Model T were to Detroit. Founded in 1871, the Beckwith Co. gained national recognition through sales of its popular "Round Oak" heating stove, considered to be the best quality heating stove – and certainly the best selling – in the United States. Unique at the time, the Round Oak could provide as much or as little heat as you wished, and would burn any kind of wood or coal. The stove was economical to operate, durable, looked good in the home, and provided clean heat. For the distinctive Dowagiac final touch, a likeness of the fictional Chief Doe-Wah-Jack was created and added to each Round Oak stove sold.

The world's most popular and most collected antique artificial fishing lure would be the ones manufactured by Dowagiac native James Heddod. James carved his first artificial fishing lure, in the shape of a frog, in the late-1890s while waiting for a friend to go fishing. That same day, he fastened hooks to his hand carved frog, tossed it into the water and caught a bass. James only carved lures in the shape of frogs for himself and for a few friends, and these are among his most rare and sought after lures, with only eight known to exist today. Sensing the great business opportunity, James and his two sons began building lures in Mrs. Heddod's kitchen in Dowagiac, and were granted their first patent in 1902. The preference for Heddod lures by generations of anglers since 1902 has made the company a success through the end of Heddod family involvement in 1955 & beyond.

Sources: Wikipedia, www.antiquefishinglures.com, *The Dowagiac Book* by Bayles & Milner, *Windows to the Past, Volumes I & II* by Stan Hamper

THE TAVERN: WOUNDED MINNOW SALOON

For the perfect ending to a perfect day on the Dowagiac River, travel 4 and 1/2 miles south of Doe-Wah-Jack's Canoe Rental to 236 S. Front Street in downtown Dowagiac. You've arrived for an evening at the Wounded Minnow Saloon, proprietor Kyle Blue.

The Wounded Minnow is a tavern tribute to James Heddod, inventor of the artificial fishing lure. When the Heddod factory in Dowagiac was closed, the bar purchased every lure that was available for sale. These lures, along with Heddod Co. posters, cover the bar walls. Even the bar menu announces all things Heddod: "Heddod surface bait produce smashes!" is one of the old newspaper headlines reproduced on the menus.

Diversions besides Heddod history are plentiful with video games, darts, pool table, pinball, and big screen TV. The bar host live entertainment on the weekends. Their outdoor seating is a nice option.

Fish 'n Chips, chicken fingers, Ugly Burgers (their name, not ours) & calzones were the items devoured by our hungry 8-person crack research team. The result: 16 thumbs up!

This tavern review ends with a bad news, good news story. The bad news: we were informed that the Wounded Minnow had run out of Pabst. The good news: the fine folks of Dowagiac apparently have extraordinarily good taste.

GRAND RIVER ONONDAGA, MICHIGAN

CANOE LIVERY:
Grand Adventures
owner Russ Bodell
4590 Onondaga Road, Onondaga Mi 49264.
Phone (517) 712-6475
no website.
Take 127 south from Lansing OR north from Jackson to the Bellevue Road/Leslie exit, go west 6 miles to the 1st stop sign, turn left on to Onondaga Road & go ¼ mile and take a right at the last drive before the river.

RIVER QUOTE:
Livery owner Russ was asked if the high water would allow us sufficient room to float beneath the 2 river bridges, "Yeah, they're new bridges." (?)

Grand River

Level Two
Intermediate Ability Required

THE BACKGROUND: GRAND RIVER

Jerry Reed sang, "You can sure get lost in the Loo-siana Bayou", and we did at one point on this trip. The Grand is Michigan's longest river, flowing 260 miles as it meanders from its' source just south of Jackson, until it empties into Lake Michigan at Grand Haven. Interestingly – especially for a 41 degree day – this great northern river took on a distinctly southern flavor on this early-April day: the combination of the normally high spring water levels, added with the meltdown of '07 – '08's unusually snowy winter season, had the river running 5' higher than normal, and it seemed that the Louisiana Bayou had taken a detour well north. The majority of the shore was underwater for today's trip, so much so that even the trees on the high ground appeared to be growing right out of the river. We could look

through these trees and their watery bases, seeing no land at all, to where the main body of the river flows on the flooded land's opposite bank. Taking a short cut through these trees and over flooded land was often an option. As I list the river's key landmarks, please note that many creeks, fallen trees, etcetera, normally seen during a mid-summer trip were underwater today.

The Grand River, for years before the Europeans arrived, was the most frequently used Native American transportation route in the area that would become Michigan. The Grand's Indian name is "O-wash-ta-nong", meaning far-away-water, a name well-suited to a 260-mile long river. As you would expect from the state's longest river, the Grand flows pasts many interesting cities and sites. The list of cities includes Jackson, Lansing, Grand Rapids, and Grand Haven. One of the interesting sites that you can float by on the river's journey to Lake Michigan is the baseball home of the West Michigan Whitecaps. Their park, known as Fifth Third Field, is in Grand Rapids. If you time your trip right, you could canoe the Grand, pull your boat over near Fifth Third Field, and see a minor league baseball game in action.

The first 2008 customers at Grand Adventures were Ethan Blake, Kenny Umphrey, Chris Weaks, Pat Kennedy, and me.

THE RIVER: PADDLING THE GRAND

The suggested trip, 10 river miles & 2 hours 25 minutes long (an estimated 3 hours at normal water levels), begins at Tompkins Road and ends at the Grand Adventures' road in the town of Onondaga. The river on this stretch flows primarily north and just a bit west. There are two public toilets along this float: at the Tompkins Road put it and at Baldwin County Park on the left shore, 10 minutes before the take out point.

10 min. in/2 hrs 15 min. to go: from the right shore, a fallen tree covers two-thirds of the river with passing space on the left. Just downstream, on a straightaway, another fallen tree from the right shore allows only a small opening to canoe through on the far left.

15 min. in/2 hrs 10 min. to go: after a big bend to the left sits a white house on the right shore. *Educational footnote*: my canoe mate, Pat Kennedy, informed me that the small green structure next door houses a wood-fired boiler that heats the white house by circulating heated water through the house.

Pat's view of how the river ran today: "Looking ahead, you wouldn't know what the definition of the river is. It looks like one big swamp."

38 min./1 hr. 37 min. to go: a bat home sits above the middle of the river on a tree leaning in from the right shore. 2 minutes downstream, a creek on the left serves as the upstream border of a stone basement home, the first of 3 side-by-side-by-side homes on the left shore. The last of the 3 homes is framed by 2 white sycamore trees, leaning into the Grand at a 45 degree angle.

1 hr. 10 min. in/1 hr. 15 min. to go: fallen trees from the right shore create back-to-back obstacles. Stick to the far left.

1 hr. 15 min. in/1 hr. 10 min. to go: you'll float beneath high tension power lines. Just downstream from the power lines are many fallen trees. Pass to their left.

Kenny Sez:
"Step out of your rut and step in a canoe."

1 hr. 30 min. in/55 min. to go: a big creek flows in from the left, bringing sufficient added volume to widen the river.

1 hr. 40 min. in/45 min. to go: here's where we got lost in the Loo-siana Bayou. With the shore below the water line, and the trees in the river's path as thick as those on what used to be the shore, we did get momentarily lost in the swamp. It was only when we stopped paddling, ensuring that the current was no longer with us, did we change course to regain the main body of the river. These are the fun moments you miss when you float at normal river levels.

1 hr. 55 min. in/30 min. to go: an unseen (on this stretch) dam downstream begins to slow the Grand as it further widens and deepens. The river starts to run a little straighter.

2 hrs 5 min. in/20 min. to go: another large creek merges from the left. 5 minutes beyond, you pass a home that sits on the right bank.

2 hrs 15 min. in/10 min. to go: Baldwin County Park is on your left. The park includes   restrooms, kid's play area, a pavilion, picnic tables, and a baseball diamond.

2 hrs 20 min. in/5 min. to go: the railroad bridge is followed immediately by the Onondaga Street auto bridge. 2 minutes downstream, you float under the 2nd auto bridge.

2 hrs 25 min. in/the end: take out on the right bank, back at Grand Adventures.

THE TOWN: JACKSON

Detroit Tigers local radio affiliate: WIBM 1450AM (Jackson).

The city of Jackson lies just north of where the Grand River has its origin, and 20 minutes south of Onondaga. Reaching across the aisle, politically-speaking, seems to have had its beginnings in Jackson. When the town was established in 1829, it was named after the newly-elected Democratic Party President, Andrew "Old Hickory" Jackson. In 1854, with Abe Lincoln in attendance, Jackson became the birthplace of the Republican Party. A historical marker located in downtown Jackson at Second and Franklin streets reads:

On July 6, 1854, a state convention of anti-slavery men was held in Jackson to found a new political party. "Uncle Tom's Cabin" had been published two years earlier, causing increased resentment against slavery, and the Kansas-Nebraska Act of May 1854 threatened to make slave states out of previously free territories. Since the convention day was hot & the huge crowd could not be accommodated in the hall, the meeting adjourned to an oak grove on "Morgan's Forty" on the outskirts of town. Here a state-wide slate of candidates was selected and the Republican Party was born. Winning an overwhelming victory in the elections of 1854, the Republican Party went on to dominate national politics throughout the nineteenth century.

Jackson is the birthplace of not only a major political party, but also an interesting mix of people: Jack Paar - original host of the Tonight Show, Tom Monaghan - Domino's Pizza founder, NASA astronauts James McDivitt /Apollo 9 commander and Alfred Worden / Apollo 15 command module pilot, Potter Stewart - U.S. Supreme Court Justice (while reviewing a pornography case came up with the famous line, "I know it when I see it"), Austin Blair - Michigan Governor during the Civil War (supported voting rights for women and for blacks when it was a radical thing to do), and a surprising number of big names in the sports world including Tony Dungy - Super Bowl winning coach, Karach Kiraly - volleyball Olympic gold medalist, & Vid Marvin – Mobil Lounge softball team leadoff man for a quarter-century and counting.

Sources: www.whitehouse.gov, Michigan historical marker, Wikipedia

THE TAVERN: ARCHEY'S

In tiny downtown Onondaga, Archey's is a 2-minute drive from the Grand Adventures canoe livery. They have a fine bar to belly up to, although we relaxed post-float at a table away from the bar, beneath the "19th Hole" sign. Archey's is a little smoky and a lot friendly. Banter with the regulars stationed up at the bar was easy with plenty of laughs. The burgers & sandwiches ordered received unanimous thumbs up from our canoe team. Always a sure sign of quality, Pabst Blue Ribbon longnecks are an everyday item at Archey's. Both of Michigan's Big Daddy universities are supported at Archey's (sure to spark a debate or two): a large U of M sign is behind the bar, and MSU's sports news is reported on Lansing State Journals posted in the restrooms. A big screen TV, pool table, and video game are all a part of a visit with the friendly folks at Archey's.

HERSEY RIVER
HERSEY, MICHIGAN

RIVER SOUNDTRACK:
Cool Water – Sons Of The Pioneers, *Crossroads* – Cream,
Jammin' – Bob Marley (from the "Captain Ron" soundtrack),
Talking Fishing Blues – Woody Guthrie,
Cool Jerk – The Capitols

CANOE LIVERY:
Hersey Canoe Livery
owner Donn Trites
625 E. 4th Street, Hersey MI 49639
Phone (231) 832-7220
www.herseycanoe.com.
(note: Donn also services the Muskegon River
with his Sawmill Canoe Livery out of Big
Rapids, Mi. Phone (231) 796-6408
www.sawmillmi.com)

RIVER QUOTE:
Marquis Weaks, "There's too many
Gilligans & not enough Gingers."

Level Two
Intermediate Ability Required

THE BACKGROUND: HERSEY RIVER

The Hersey River is a 21 mile long river, with its headwaters beginning just south of Leroy, approximately 10 miles to the north of the junction of US10 & US131 at the town of Reed City. The Hersey flows south and southwesterly as it crosses US131 6 miles north of Reed City, then turns straight south while running along the western edge of US131. Two miles north of Reed City, the Hersey turns southeast and again crosses over US131 & then US10 on its way through Reed City. 4 miles downstream from Reed City, the Hersey River flows through the heart of downtown Hersey. At the end of its journey through the town of Hersey, the river ends as it merges with the 230-mile long mighty Muskegon River.

The suggested Hersey River trip could not have been made before 2007, as this stretch of the river was blocked by the Hersey Dam, located just before the confluence of the Hersey and Muskegon Rivers. This dam was built in 1858, and has been slowly falling into disrepair since the 1940s. The economic benefits of the dam had long since ceased to exist, and the dam was removed in November 2006. With the dam gone, several of the Hersey's 21 miles have been opened not only to paddlers, but also to fishermen: the Hersey is considered one of the finest coldwater fisheries in the Midwest and, before the lumbermen ravaged it in the 1880s and 1890s, was bursting with trout. The DNR would like to return the Hersey to the blue ribbon trout stream that it once was. Based on the experiences of livery employee Eric, they're well on their way. Eric told us that he has landed some of the biggest trout that he's ever caught while fishing this river.

Sources: U.S Fish & Wildlife Journal, Detroit Free Press, www.glhabitant. org, Donn Trites

The Hersey River Paddlers and Wildlife Spotting Team included Tyler, Cam, Paige, Kim & Perry VerMerris, Katrina & Captain Johnny Harcourt, and me.

THE RIVER: PADDLING THE HERSEY

The suggested trip is a short one and the only one available in 2008, taking our paddlers only 1 hour and 11 minutes. Although the dam removal has opened up the last 7 miles of the Hersey River before its merger with the Muskegon River, there are 2 factors that limit use of all 7 miles, and both factors will be less of an issue over time:

1)   lack of public access points (this problem is being worked on) and
2)   cattle guards are stretched across the river, upstream from today's put in point. As it was explained it to me, cows mosey on down to the river to drink water and, at times, wander in too far & get swept downstream. Thus the need for the cattle guards. Plans are in place to remove these. Not only will this allow longer floats down the Hersey, but may lead to interesting river conversations as well:

"Say Bob, do you remember what river we're on today?"

"Well Bill, I just saw Elsie float by, so I have to assume that we're on the Hersey"

"Thanks Bob".

This abbreviated adventure includes a campground, the one at Blodgett Park (2 minutes from the trip's end), and two locations with bathrooms: at the Hersey Main Street Bridge park (43 minutes after the put in) and at Blodgett Park.

The put in point is at the Albright Methodist Camp. Here the river is 25' to 30' across, and 2' deep. The river floor is a mix of sand, gravel, and rocks.

7 min. in / 1 hr. 4 min. to go: Float beneath a foot bridge. On the approach to the bridge, the river shallows to 6" deep.

12 min. in / 59 min. to go: Beyond a stone island, left of midstream, float under power lines. One deer and one fawn on shore watch us float by with enough interest not to run away. Beyond the power lines, as the river bends left, you encounter the first set of light rapids. Happily, you will see many such rapids today. 1 minute downstream, you'll pass between concrete supports of a lost bridge.

18 min. in / 53 min. to go: Conclude 4 consecutive bends of FUN light rapids! 5 minutes downstream is a beautiful home where the river bends right, then a brief but thoroughly enjoyable light rapids run.

It was about this point when Johnny began quoting Kurt Russell's finest character, Captain Ron ("Your boat sank?" "No, not my boat, my boss's boat. We hit this reef – huge son of a bitch, ran the whole coast" "Wait. The Great Barrier Reef?" "You heard of it? Smart lady") 27 min. in / 44 min. to go: Mid-stream sits an island of driftwood. Passing on its left, float through a nice little ripple run & tiny chops on the bottom of the canoe.

It seems as though you're never more than a few bends from a fine light rapids run. This is really a fun river! The Hersey River is also rich in driftwood. Do stay alert as there is a good deal of submerged or partially-submerged logs that you will want to avoid getting friendly with.

Kenny Sez: "The grass may be greener on the other side 'cause there are more cow pies over there "

34 min. in / 37 min. to go: Nice break spot shows itself on the left shore, right after the river bends to the left. This is a 20' long sandy beach, about 4' wide. The river here is shallow with a sandy bottom – a fine Frisbee area. 1 minute downstream, a loud spring flows into the Hersey from your right.

43 min. in / 28 min. to go: As the Main Street Bridge in the town of Hersey comes into view, you enter a rocky run with quite a bit of white water. Just beyond the bridge, on the right, is a park with outhouses, picnic tables, and grills. As you pass the park, the river develops a long stretch of water with a nice chop to it.

58 min. in / 13 min. to go: The river bends right where the small cabin sits on the left bank. Here, the river becomes extremely shallow and rocky, and fast whitewater develops. Hug the left shore to avoid the larger rocks in the river's middle and right. Along the left shore is also where the river is deepest, minimizing the likelihood that you have to walk your canoe through.

1 hr. 3 min. in / 8 min. to go: Just like 5 minutes earlier, here's another extremely shallow and rocky stretch with fast whitewater. Again, stay to the left as your best bet to avoid a walk through.

1 hr. 7 min. in / 4 min. to go: A short rapids run takes you to the end of a straightaway, and up to a small grassy island on the river's right. The river performs a cool looking snake left around the island.

1 hr. 9 min. in / 2 min. to go: Marked by a fishing pier extending out into the river, on the river's right shore, is Blodgett Park. This excellent park has bathrooms and other amenities detailed under "The Towns" section.

1 hr. 10 min. in / 1 min. to go: From your left, here comes the 140' wide Muskegon River, and its junction with the Hersey River.

1 hour and 11 minutes in, and you're at the trip's end. Take the turnout on the right, before the bridge.

THE TOWNS: REED CITY & HERSEY

Detroit Tigers local radio affiliate: WDEE 97.3FM (Reed City/Big Rapids).

Reed City: Sitting on the banks of the Hersey River, Reed City also goes by the name of "Crossroads" for 3 very good reasons, with reasons 2 and 3 direct descendants of the 1st: (1) in the town's early days (1880s – 1890s), as it prospered during the logging heyday, Reed City was a major transportation hub, with rail lines and roads running east & west and north & south through town, (2) Reed City sits at the intersection of two important highways, US10 & US131, and (3) in the heart of downtown is the junction of two major trails in the state's "rails-to-trails" system, the White Pine and the Pere Marquette trails. The White Pine Trail runs 92 miles, from Cadillac in the north to Comstock Park (north Grand Rapids) in the south. The P.M. Trail is a work in progress that will run 95 miles from Midland in the east to Baldwin in the west. These are two wonderful trails for walking, hiking, and biking - and Reed City, with its rebuilt old railroad depot acting as the hub where the two trails meet, is in the heart of it all.

Novelist Jim Harrison was raised in Reed City. Jim's writing is often compared to that of Hemingway, and many of his stories are set in Michigan..His work has appeared in *The New York Times Magazine*, *Sports Illustrated, Esquire, Playboy,* and *Rolling Stone*. His novels include three which were made into movies, "Wolf", Revenge", and "Legends of the Fall". "The Theory & Practice of Rivers" is a book of Jim's poems, with the title poem comparing life and death to a river journey, and the whole work serving as a collection of memories of people and of rivers from his past.

Sources: The Northern Camper, www.reedcitycrossroads.com, Wikipedia, Publisher's Weekly

Hersey: Both the towns of Hersey and Reed City are found within Osceola County. Osceola County's first European resident, arriving in the 1840s, was Doc Blodgett. Doc first arrived in town at the confluence of the Hersey River and the Muskegon River, the spot of what is now Blodgett Landing. Blodgett Landing is the jewel of the village of Hersey. This beautiful park has modern camp sites, a bathhouse, two picnic pavilions, & a playground area with a volleyball court. The two rivers provide folks with opportunities to swim, canoe, kayak, tube, and to toss in a line off of the fishing pier. For those who'd like to bicycle, a paved section of the Pere Marquette Trail (rails-to-trails) is just ¼ mile from the Landing. Additional paths for walking are located throughout the park.

The village is undergoing a trinity renaissance: the growing popularity – well beyond the town itself – of Blodgett Landing, the removal of the dam and the resulting opening up of the Hersey River, and the completion of the new Main Street Bridge (the western view of the Hersey River from this new bridge is spectacular).

Osceola County is 40 miles east of Lake Michigan and rich in timber. With an elevation 400' above that of Lake Michigan, and rivers flowing downhill to the Big Lake, the county was well-positioned to be prosperous during the late-1800s logging days.

To complete the circle of this Hersey River story: first county resident Doc Blodgett donated some of his 1800s timber riches for the construction of the Albright Methodist Camp – the camp that served as the launch point for this Hersey River float.

Sources: "One Hundred Going On Two Hundred" by Marjorie Brown White, Donn Trites, www.herseycanoe.com

THE TAVERN: BROTHERS BAR & GRILL REED CITY

I like this bar. A very comfortable feeling is palatable here. The bar is Brothers, located in downtown Reed City, 4 miles northwest of our Hersey River take out point. One of the first things that you notice at Brothers are the tables: beneath clear laminated table tops are sports cards, baseball cards at one table, football cards at another, and other tables each featuring hockey, basketball, and auto racing. Pizza AND Pabst longnecks!?! I could stay a <u>bit</u> longer. A series of dead critters stick their heads and antlers through the walls above you (the comfortable feeling might not be quite so palatable to these animals), while big screen TVs and sports memorabilia cover the walls below. Through the back door is outdoor seating where there's music playing. And then there was our wonderfully-feisty waitress, a cousin of the two brothers who own the bar, "I'm Lisa. Unless I have a complaint. Then I'm Julie". I'm still laughing.

KALAMAZOO RIVER
SAUGATUCK, MICHIGAN

RIVER QUOTE:
Doc regarding the impressive river width, "I half expect to see Detroit on my right and Windsor on my left."

RIVER SOUNDTRACK:
Twenty Miles From Shore – Hawkshaw Hawkins,
Summer Breeze – Maitries
I Got a Gal in Kalamazoo – Glenn Miller
Singapore Silk Torpedo – Pretty Things
Ghost Town – The Specials

CANOE LIVERY:
Old Allegan Canoe
owners Kathey and Jim Bailey
2722 Old Allegan Road, Fennville MI 49408
Phone (269) 561-5481
www.oldallegancanoe.com.
(2nd location: Kayakers Run
110 Water St., Plainwell MI 49080
269-685-1139)

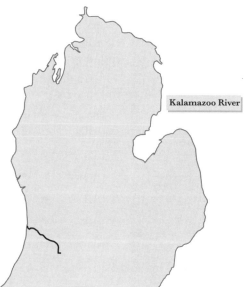

Kalamazoo River

Level One
Beginner Ability Required

THE BACKGROUND: KALAMAZOO RIVER

The Kalamazoo River runs for 166 miles, with its headwaters just southwest of Jackson. The river runs in a northwesterly direction, flowing through towns including Albion, Marshall, Battle Creek, Kalamazoo, and Saugatuck before it ends at Lake Michigan.

As livery owner and van driver Kathey pulled up with our crack research team to today's river put in point, we were immediately struck by the width of the Kalamazoo, at least as wide as any section of any river canoed for this book. Despite its impressive girth, you still wouldn't think that you could hide a town beneath it – which leads us to the tale of "The Lost City of Singapore"…

Beneath the sands near the mouth of the Kalamazoo River, where the river empties into Lake Michigan, lie the ruins of Michigan's most famous ghost town, Singapore. The town of Singapore sat just downriver from and north of Saugatuck, on the northernmost bend of the Kalamazoo River. The town was founded in 1836 by New York land speculators hoping to rival Chicago and Milwaukee as a lake port. Singapore was, until 1871, a busy lumbering town. With 3 mills, 2 hotels, several general stores, an infamous "Wildcat" bank, and home to Michigan's first schoolhouse, it outshone its neighbor to the south, "The Flats", as Saugatuck was then called. In 1871, the worst recorded fire in U.S. history ravaged the towns of Chicago, Peshtigo (Wisconsin), and the Michigan towns of Holland and Manistee. In a strange turn of events, the great fire of 1871 brought Singapore both riches and her demise.

Much of the lumber needed to rebuild the fire ravaged towns was purchased from the mills of Singapore. In order to supply such great quantities of lumber, the town was almost completely deforested. Without the protective tree cover, the winds and sands coming off of Lake Michigan quickly eroded Singapore into ruins. By 1875, the town was vacated (many residents moved to The Flats, i.e. Saugatuck) and completely covered over by sand drifts. Today Singapore is buried beneath the dunes.

Sources: Michigan Historic Site marker, Singapore: Michigan's Imaginary Pompeii by Charles R. Starring

The Kalamazoo River research team: Ron Swiecki and Ronnie Jr., Tommy Holbrook, Theresa Melching, Bret Holbrook, Kanoo Kenny Umphrey, his grandson Ethan Chandler Blake, and me.

THE RIVER: PADDLING THE KALAMAZOO

The suggested trip ran our group just under 3 hours. The 8 and one-half mile trip begins at the Ottawa Marsh put in, at 128th and 46th roads. As we launch, crack researcher Kenny estimates that the river is running "20 canoe lengths wide". Kathey Bailey's river width estimate is 200' wide. The consensus: this is one wide river! The water is deeper than the length of our canoe paddles, and will range today from 8' deep to rare spots where you drag bottom. The trip passes no authorized campgrounds and no toilets.

16 min. in / 2 hrs 38 min. to go: On the right bank is a 30' wide, access-friendly dirt slope, making for a fine pull over spot. At the end of the long straight-away on which the slope sits is an 80' tall sand dune that stretches for a spell as the river bends left.

26 min. in / 2 hrs 28 min. to go: **Stay to the right!** Marked by a 3' tall by 12' wide concrete slab on the left bank, there's a major fork in the river. To the left is a marsh. The river flows to the right.

36 min. in / 2 hrs 18 min. to go: Small grassy island hugs the right shore and makes for a good break spot. We have our first of several blue heron sightings.

41 min. in / 2 hrs 13 min. to go: Dead creek merges from the right. At straight-away's end is another towering sand dune where the river bends left.

57 min. in / 1 hr. 57 min. to go: Excellent Frisbee location, where the river bends left. The river is 6" deep, 120' across, and the river floor is obstacle-free.

1 hour in / 1 hr. 54 min. to go: Bat house on a small island near the right shore.

1 hr. 15 min. in / 1 hr. 39 min. to go: Another beautiful Frisbee area where the river bends right and a creek rolls in from the left. Ronnie says, "It's the largest Frisbee spot we've ever seen!"

1 hr. 30 min. in / 1 hr. 24 min. to go: The half-way point of the trip is well-marked with a great break location: 100' long beach fronted by yet another fabulous Frisbee spot (the frequency of the great Frisbee areas is one of the Kalamazoo River's finest gifts). A blue heron poses for a photo.

Kenny Sez: "The Kalamazoo River, where 2-year old cheese and 4-year old crackers taste good together."

1 hr. 48 min. in / 1 hr. 6 min. to go: "Bill's Bench" can be seen on the right bank. 1 minute downstream, a wide creek merges from your left. 4 minutes beyond the creek, a dirt road comes up to the river's edge from the right.

1 hr. 55 min. in / 1 hour to go: One hour to go is marked with two long, good looking break spots, two minutes and one fallen tree apart, and both with a friendly slope for pullovers. A bend or two past the 2nd break spot, homes are seen for the first time (there's a gorgeous home alongside a merging creek).

2 hrs 10 min. in / 44 min. to go: "Drenton's River Rats" reads the sign along the right shore fronting a home. During the drought of 2007, low water uncovered an island in front of this house. The island was decorated by the locals with tiki torches and a sign reading "Beer Island". Many '07 paddlers lengthen their river float with a visit to Beer Island, bringing new meaning to the word "sandbar".

2 hrs 16 min. in / 38 min. to go: Dolphin sighting… just before the river breaks left, a thick log that will not be moving anytime soon sits midstream. Ronnie Junior believes the log resembles a dolphin. After the left river bend, a large beach is on the left shore.

2 hrs 25 min. in / 28 min. to go: There's less than a half-hour to go when you float under the power lines. 5 minutes downstream is a 2nd set of power lines.

2 hrs 37 min. in / 17 min. to go: The river bends left, revealing a 150' long beach. Four minutes beyond, a 50' wide creek with a strong current merges from the right.

2 hrs 44 min. in / 10 min. to go: Nice homes! At the end of a long straight-away where the river bends right, a home on a high bluff features a very cool stairway leading to the water. Looking down a big creek to the left is a majestic-looking home. A blue heron flies ahead of us.

2 hours and 54 minutes, and you're in. With the take-out point in sight, float beneath two side-by-side bridges, then exit right at the large ramp at Old Allegan Road (at 58th Street).

THE TOWN: SAUGATUCK

Detroit Tigers local radio affiliate: WHTC 1450 AM (Holland)

Before the first settlers arrived, Saugatuck was a part of the Potawatomi Indian Nation that spanned southern Michigan and northern Indiana. Up until 1830, the only humans seen other than Indians were French Voyageurs who trapped for furs and traded with the Indians. The first area settler was William Butler who, in 1830, platted a village on a small level area at the foot of a clay bluff. The village contour inspired its early name, "The Flats".

Blessed as the area was with pine trees, the lumbering era was very good to The Flats. The town experienced tremendous growth as Midwest towns purchased their white pines to rebuild in the wake of the 1871 fire. The Flats became a noisy neighborhood as lumberjacks, flush with cash, joined sailors to pack the ever-increasing number of taverns that were opening. New home construction was taking place on the high ground, away from The Flats rowdiness. As the area lumber boom wound down in the 1880s, fruit growing replaced lumber to drive the economy. In Chicago, Michigan peaches were in demand, referred to there as "Michigan Gold", and one-quarter of Michigan peaches came from (the town now known as) Saugatuck and neighboring Douglas. The local economy was further buoyed by growth in shipping and in boat building. Many Saugatuck homes built at that time by folks in the shipping or boat building business still stand today.

The artistic, tourist, and resort Saugatuck of today emerged at the turn of the last century, when a group of Chicago artists established in 1910 the "Summer School of Paintings". Nationally-known artists began to make their summer homes in Saugatuck, with the town on the road to being known as the "Art Coast of Michigan". The strong artistic presence has been, and continues to be, a big factor in making tourism the town's primary industry.

Today, Saugatuck is well-recognized for its cool. Recently, *Midwest Living Magazine* ranked Saugatuck/Douglas fifth among the top 100 vacation destinations in the Midwest. *Life Magazine* chose Saugatuck as the "Best Dune Town" and one of the eight most perfect summer getaways. Saugatuck and Douglas were two of only 28 communities awarded the "Preserve America Community" designation by the White House in 2004.

Saugatuck's Oval Beach has received high praise from a wide variety of sources: *Conde Nast's Traveler Magazine* has rated it one of the 25 best shorelines in the world, *MTV* rated the beach one of the top 5 in America, *National Geographic Traveler Magazine* placed it within the top 2 U.S. beaches, and the *Chicago Tribune* ranks Oval Beach among the top 5 in the Midwest. *Screen Actor's Guild Magazine* ranks the top 3 film festivals in the world as 1. Sundance, 2. Cannes Film Festival, and 3. Saugatuck's Waterfront Film Festival. For 4 days each June since 1999, Saugatuck becomes one big street party as thousands of residents and tourists mingle with some of the best film directors, actors, writers, producers, and the industry's biggest celebrities. Capturing the feel of the event were comments by former MGM Vice President Jay Froberg: "It's an amazing opportunity to throw on your flip-flops and stroll to see a movie that the world hasn't discovered yet". Sources: Wikipedia, www.preserveamerica.gov, A Tour of Saugatuck History brochure, Saugatuck/Douglas Visitors Guide

THE TAVERN: WALLY'S BAR & GRILL

"They don't have pizza? What kind of bar and grill is this?"

Despite these wise words of 8-year old Ronnie Junior, we decided to drink and dine at Wally's, anyway. It is located in the heart of downtown Saugatuck at 128 Hoffman Street, 15 minutes from the Old Allegan Canoe Livery in Fennville. Wally's is as close as this town gets to blue collar, a place, we were told, where the bartenders and wait staff from other local bars go for their fun.

Making a fan of baseball and its history comfortable is Wally's Men's Room. Let me rephrase that. It's the fact that the bar's Men's Room is identified as such not by the words "Men's Room" or "Men", but rather by a photo of George Sisler on the Men's Room door. *Side note*: George's 257 hits in 1920 stood as the Major League Baseball record for hits in a season until Ichiro's 262 in 2004.

So, what we have here is no pizza (or pool tables, darts, video games), but George Sisler and Pabst Blue Ribbon longnecks, always a sure sign of quality. We can make this work. Everyone said they liked the food that they ordered, including burgers and fresh perch.

The majority of Wally's seating is outdoors, offering an excellent vantage point for you to watch Saugatuck walk by. Beyond the dining area, you can grab a bar stool and belly up to either the outdoor or the indoor bar. I struck up conversations with barkeeps at both the inside and outside bar, and I was impressed by their friendliness & pleasant attitudes.

The outdoor bar's backdrop is a large wooden arch with beautiful detail work. The barkeep told me that, in 2004, it took 30 guys to carry it into Wally's. He believed that it was built in Illinois around 100 years ago, forgotten about, somehow ended up in a Missouri warehouse where it was found a few years back and purchased for Wally's.

LOOKING GLASS RIVER PORTLAND, MICHIGAN

RIVER QUOTE:
Pam, "Even a bad day on the river is better than a good day at the office."

RIVER SOUNDTRACK:
I'm Walkin' – Fats Domino
Rock & Roll Music – the Frost
Quiet Village – Martin Denny
It Don't Mean A Thing (If It Ain't Got That Swing) – Duke Ellington
Hold On I'm Comin' – Sam & Dave (Isaac Hayes tribute)

CANOE LIVERY:
Wacousta Canoe Livery
owner Betty Harlow
9988 Riverside Dr., Eagle MI 48822
Phone (517) 626-6873
no website
Directions: I-96 exit 90, left at end of exit ramp on to Grand River, go 2 miles to Wacousta Road. Turn right and travel 1.5 miles to Riverside (at beautiful red barn) and turn left, follow to last house on the right.

Looking Glass River

Level Two
Intermediate Ability Required

THE BACKGROUND: LOOKING GLASS RIVER

"Smooth it slides upon its travel, Here a wimple, there a gleam –
O the clean gravel! O the smooth stream!"

So goes the first lines from Robert Louis Stevenson's poem, *The Looking Glass River*. A float down the Looking Glass indicates that Mister Stevenson experienced this river first hand, and a fortunate man that he was. Deeply beautiful reflections off of the river's surface, as the water gently ripples over rocks, treat you to a visual paradise throughout. All along the banks of the Looking Glass River are Native American burial grounds of the Wacousta (wah-coo-sta) Tribe. The meandering 65 miles of the Looking Glass ends at its confluence with the Grand River in downtown Portland. Can I get an "amen?"

During our late-August float, the water was very low. The kayaks fared well, but the canoes continually ran aground. In our canoe, on 12 occasions one or both of us were required to get out of the canoe and push it to deeper water in order to continue. Please, do not let this low water story stop you from paddling down the Looking Glass, because this is a river that should not be missed. Just remember, if it's late in the season, stick with a kayak for your Looking Glass journey.

The Looking Glass Bottom-Bumpers: Gloria Miller, Pam Fleming, Carol Poenish, Star, Gilda Weaks, Marquis Weaks, Pat Marten, Darryl T Couch, Andy Kocembo, Paula Brown, Chris Weaks, Tommy Holbrook, Maggie & me.

THE RIVER: PADDLING THE LOOKING GLASS

The suggested trip ran 4 hours (estimated by the livery at 3 to 3.5 hours during normal, higher, water levels). We launched at the Lowell Bridge, with the trip end at Wacousta Canoe Livery. **Key landmarks**: approx. 1 hour in is the Frances Road Bridge, approx. 2 hours in is the Herbison Road Bridge, at 2 hours and 45 minutes is Heritage Park, and 30 minutes downstream from Heritage Park is the Looking Glass Valley Park (43 minutes from the take out). Restrooms are found at Heritage Park & Looking Glass Valley Park.

The Looking Glass trip begins with the river running 1.5' deep and 30' wide. On the banks and in the river, rocks are everywhere, running up to 2' in diameter, and many have been aluminized (i.e. kissed a few canoes). Some rocks are just below the water line, some just above.

8 min. in / 3 hr. 52 min. to go: A good-sized creek merges from your left. There's a great deal of bottom-skimming occurring. 4 minutes downstream, hug the right shore to avoid the fallen tree.

20 min. in / 3 hrs 40 min. to go: A long string of islands lie midstream. The river picks up speed as you snake past tangles of branches and fallen trees extending into the water from both riverbanks. Just downstream, a <u>very</u> large uprooted tree blocks the river flow from midstream to the left bank, leaving an arch to float under on the right.

Trees form a cooling canopy during long stretches of the trip, turning the thermostat down 10 degrees on a high-80 degree day.

35 min. in / 3 hrs 25 min. to go: Fallen tree from the right shore blocks the entire river except for a 7' gap on the left bank.

40 min. in / 3 hrs 20 min. to go: A creek joining the river from the right precedes by 5 minutes a visually striking sight: the Looking Glass River's version of Beijing's "Bird's Nest" Olympic Stadium. You'll know it when you see it (to quote Maggie, "the spirits of the Indians were angry that day, my friends"). Completely crossing the river are fallen trees from the left bank. Approaching from a distance, there appears to be no way to paddle through. To pass, stay slightly right of midstream then veer back left.

53 min. in / 3 hrs 7 min. to go: Big uprooted tree leaning in low from the left shore, with its base 12' tall & perpendicular to the ground, blocks left passage around a small island.

57 min. in / 3 hrs 3 min. to go: Float beneath the Frances Road Bridge, the first bridge since the Lowell Road Bridge put in. Livery help Zeb, Dave, & Zack told us that the river was so high during the Spring, there was not enough space to paddle a canoe below the Frances Road Bridge. There was plenty of room to float beneath in late-August.

1 hr. in / 3 hrs to go: The 10' tall exposed base of an uprooted tree sits along the right bank. To the left of this tree is a very shallow walk-through. 100 yards downstream a fallen tree blocks the entire river. The water was low enough, on the far right, to push rider-less canoes below the arch of the fallen tree.

Swimming by us all day long were large schools of fish including rock bass, smallmouth bass, largemouth bass, and carp. The great amounts of feeder fish spoke to the excellent health of the river: the bait was not working as there were too many tasty minnows for the fish to feed on. Not being a fisherman, but being a pizza lover, the best analogy that I could come up with was, why eat warmed up frozen pie when fresh, homemade, hot, and straight out of the oven pizza was right in front of their little fish faces.

1 hr. 17 min. in / 2 hrs 43 min. to go: Beautiful little creek rolls in from the left. 8 minutes downstream a small, but loud, spring merges in from the left, just before a 2nd spring.

1 hr. 24 min. in / 2 hrs 36 min. to go: Rock 7' in diameter protrudes 3' above the water line. Clam shells are scattered along the river floor. Among the wildlife are Blue Heron and muskrat sightings. 90 minutes into the trip, you begin floating through a subdivision.

1 hr. 54 min. in / 2 hrs 6 min. to go: The approximate half-way point, the Herbison Road Bridge (confirmed by the name stenciled on the middle of the bridge support), is reached.

Kenny Sez: *"I don't think that the glass is half full OR half empty. I think you just have 50% too much glass"*

2 hrs 20 min. in / 1 hr. 40 min. to go: Pretty little creek merges right, among the high banks. 1 minute downstream, the river appears to be completely blocked by debris, and by trees fallen from both shores. Pass just right of center to shoot the gap.

One of the clues that it was a bit late in the season to be canoeing this river: a riverside home owner approached us, asking if we were surveyors. "You folks surveyors? You must be surveyors. Nobody canoes the river this late in the summer."

We're encountering runs of fast water here and there.

2 hrs 45 min. in / 1 hr. 15 min. to go: Heritage Park is on your right. The park features two extremely clean and well-maintained (almost fancy) outhouses, pavilions, swing sets, kid's playscape, tennis courts, and softball diamonds. A very nice park.

Dozens of beautiful fish fly upstream past us. During the 15 minutes beyond Heritage Park, the river deepens to 2'.

3 hrs in / 1 hr. to go: The river shallows on the approach to a small island on the right – pass on the left. Follow the "v" between the next two islands for a fun little fast water rush as the river dips slightly.

3 hrs 17 min. / 43 min. to go: Looking Glass Valley Park is on your left. As with Heritage Park, this park makes a great picnic area, and includes a pavilion, volleyball courts, a kid's playscape, restrooms, and a baseball diamond. At the park's downstream end, float beneath the Wacousta Road Bridge (you are now just south of the town of Wacousta).

Note: in late-July, deer flies plagued the river. Betty Harlow said that the only effective remedy was to apply Vick's VapoRub. Those medicated vapors just don't agree with the little buggers. If the deer flies come out, and you're canoeing with a cough, you can kill two birds with one stone. Sickness never felt so good.

3 hrs 45 min. in / 15 min. to go: A baby creek flows in from the left. In another 3 minutes you pass the little fisher boy statue, fronted by a rock wall, on the right bank.

4 hours on the river, and you're in! Betty Harlow's house and livery is on your left, just before the Bauer Road Bridge.

THE TOWN: PORTLAND

Detroit Tigers local radio affiliate: WVFN 730 AM (Lansing).

"Welcome To Portland – City of Two Rivers" is the sign at the city limits, honoring two of Portland's most prized features, the Looking Glass River and the Grand River. These two meandering rivers meet in downtown Portland, 50' off of the back deck of Duke's Canoe Club (see "Taverns"), and 25 miles west of downtown Lansing. On the eastern bank of the merging rivers, a favorite Native American camp spot pre-1840s, is Two Rivers Park and its Portland Bandshell, the host location of "Thursdays on the Grand", a free summer concert series. Portland's "Riverwalk" circles the city, connects the town's parks and schools, and entices folks to get out and walk.

Within the city are 4 historic metal truss bridges, all still in use. One block south of the afore mentioned Duke's Canoe Club is the Veteran's Memorial Bridge, constructed in 1890, serving vehicular traffic and the only one of the 4 still in its original location, on Bridge Street between Water and Kent Streets over the Grand. The 2nd of the 4 bridges spans the Looking Glass River in town. A third is the Kent Street Bridge over the Grand, noteworthy for its arched shape, and visible while driving along I-96. The fourth and final bridge was formerly a railroad bridge, now converted for pedestrian use over the Grand River.

Mary Elizabeth Newman Rice, in 1837, was the first pioneer child born in Portland. From Mary's journal is the story of how Portland came to be named:

"Shortly after their arrival the settlers were called together for the purpose of naming the village so that letters might reach them more readily. My father asked my uncle Abram Hixon to go to the meeting. When it came to handing in the names there were so many that it staggered the assembly. The names suggested were Johnstown, Jamestown, Boguetown, Boyerville and Newmanville (*note*: all names of early Portland settlers). During the silence that followed, Abram Hixon said to father, "Why not call it Portland?" "Suggest it", said father, but he declined. Father then said the name of Portland had been suggested to him and he thought it very appropriate as there certainly was a fine landing where all the passing boats stopped. All present were pleased with the name and so Portland was named."

No review of the Looking Glass River and the Portland area would be complete without a few words about the First Ladies of the Looking Glass, livery owner Betty Harlow and Gloria Miller, President of the Friends of the Looking Glass…

In 1971, Mister Harlow's barber shop business began to suffer when, as Betty put it, "Everyone, including my two boys, wanted to look like the Beatles". One day that year, while sitting in her backyard on the southern shore of the Looking Glass River, Betty watched canoers float by. And the thought hit her: "Hey, I could run a livery!" And so she did, starting her Wacousta Canoe Livery with 5 canoes purchased in 1971 from… Gloria Miller.

"A river is the memory of the land through which it has passed" reads the quote on the cover of the pamphlet for the Friends of the Looking Glass, Gloria Miller - President.

The FOTLG is a volunteer group that works to educate and promote awareness of the river and its watershed, and to promote responsible land use and environmental practice within. Gloria has a passion for rivers and for their history. In 1990, to celebrate her 65th birthday, Gloria participated in the first "Grand River Expedition". The Expedition is a 20 mile per day canoe trip, covering the entire 260 mile length of the Grand River over a 13 day period. Gloria's experience with the 1990 Expedition inspired her to do something positive for the Looking Glass, the river that she grew up on. As a result, Gloria formed the Friends of the Looking Glass River in October of 1990.

10 years later, in 2000, Gloria celebrated her 75th birthday by canoeing the 260 miles of the 2nd Grand River Expedition. The 3rd Expedition will be held in 2010, coincidentally the year in which Gloria turns 85, and not so coincidentally where Gloria plans to be, and not as a spectator.

Sources: www.portland-michigan.org, Wikipedia, www.portlandmichigan.us,
Betty Harlow, Friends of the Looking Glass, Gloria Miller

THE TAVERN: DUKE'S CANOE CLUB

Also known as "Duke's Cajun Bar & Grill", Duke's sits on blessed land, immediately south of the confluence of the Looking Glass River and the Grand River. Sitting on Duke's back deck is the perfect place to look out over the merger of these two waterways, a scene so beautiful that sipping a beer other than Pabst (sadly, not available at Duke's) will do just fine.

The walls of Duke's are a place for art and expression. On the outside south wall is drawn a kokopelli flute player among the words "jazz, blues and Cajun cuisine". Inside written on the east wall are the lyrics to "When The Saints Go Marching In", on the west wall is "Laissez Les Bon Temps Roulez" – in both New Orleans and in Portland that means, "Let the Good Times Roll!" (Maggie was semi-impressed that I knew this).

"The Pointe" is the name given to Duke's back deck with a view, where we were treated to the father & son guitar duo of Darin & DJ. If that's typical of the entertainment on the deck, then the view of the rivers comes with a fine soundtrack. If you're at Duke's on a summer Thursday night, "The Pointe" music will be preceded by the music floating across the Looking Glass from the Portland Bandshell's "Thursdays on the Grand".

The dining is fine, too, featuring Duke's Chicago brick fired pizza, and Cajun items including grilled andouille sausage, pasta ala Bourbon Street, blackened alligator, and one of Newman's favorites, jambalaya (pronounced by Newman, "jum-bah-lie-ah!"). The menu includes many other items as well.

MAPLE RIVER HUBBARDSTON, MICHIGAN

RIVER SOUNDTRACK:
Kick Out The Jams – MC5
I Got My Mojo Working – Ann Cole
Magnificent Seven – Elmer Bernstein
Little Arrows – Leapy Lee
Swanee River Boogie – Albert Ammons

CANOE LIVERY:
Maple River Campground
owners Dianna & Mike Nehmer
15420 French Rd, Pewamo MI 48873
Phone (989) 981-6792
website www.michcampgrounds.com/mapleriver.
The livery is NE of Ionia and NW of St. Johns. Take M21 to Hubbardston Road, and go north 5 miles to French Road (just south the river). Turn right at French Road and follow it to the livery

RIVER QUOTE:
From livery man Dale, wearing his Michigan State University shirt, "I wouldn't pull for Michigan if they were playing Iraq"

Maple River

Level One
Beginner Ability Required

THE BACKGROUND: MAPLE RIVER

Traveling north from Lansing on US27 is a journey filled with fun landmarks. The list includes two beauties on the east side of 27: Loghenge (wooden cousin to Stonehenge) and the long rows of wind swept leaning trees. Also on that list is the crossing over the beautiful Maple River, just south of M57. The river view from US27 is one of vast, shallow, sprawling wetlands, and includes sightings of egrets, osprey, and the occasional deer wading into the water. According to the Michigan DNR, the Maple River is the largest contiguous wetland complex in mid-Michigan. The fruitless search for a livery that services the Maple ended in 2008, the year that Dianna and Mike Nehmer added a canoe livery to their campgrounds.

The Maple Rag 4 Crack Researchers: Mister P Pienta, Tommy Holbrook, Kanoo Kenny Umphrey, and me.

THE RIVER: PADDLING THE MAPLE

Suggested trip runs 1 hour and 40 minutes, putting in at the Tallman Road Bridge, and taking out at the Maple River Campground. This entire stretch of the Maple floats past state land, and a great deal of camping occurs on its flat river banks. No toilets are encountered until the outhouse on the left bank, just before the trip's end. A pair of bald eagles and a pair of blue herons are sighted on our float. The long straight-aways on the Maple River have been given the well-earned nickname of "the straights".

As you launch, the river is 4 canoe lengths wide and more than a paddle deep, according to the crack research team. The current has so little movement, that there was some question regarding which way the river runs. The answer is left, away from the Tallman Road Bridge. This is a v-e-r-r-y slow river.

Tommy noted, "This river looks like the Swanee River. I've never been on the Swanee River, but if I had, this is what it would look like." This is the type of invaluable analysis required of a crack research team member.

11 min. in / 1 hr. 29 min. to go: On the left is a long, grassy island that takes 2 minutes to paddle past. The island fronts flat ground that would make an ideal (and big!) camp or break spot. The main body of the river flows right around the island, but there's plenty of room to pass on the left, allowing easy access to the flat ground.

Just beyond the island, the river shallows to 2' deep and is a football field wide. Two minutes downstream, the river depth once again is over-your-paddle-length deep and the width tightens to 120'.

You are struck by the tremendous number of good looking camp sites that the Maple has to offer along both river banks.

Clearly seen is the high water mark on shoreline trees left from the effects of the northern edge of Hurricane Ike. During Ike's high water, the great looking campsites would've all been underwater, and all that would be seen on the banks would be trees sticking up from the water.

23 min. in / 1 hr. 17 min. to go: On the right shore, a 7' wide grassy path rises to high ground wide enough for a roomy 4-tent campsite.

The long, wide straight-aways, framed by the tall and ancient trees, have a majestic feel to them.

40 min. in / 1 hr. to go: A creek merges from the left, 15' wide at its mouth. The creek is near the beginning of an extremely long straight-away that takes 20 minutes to paddle.

The light rainfall makes me wish that I had a pair of those Norm Cash sunglasses with the battery-operated windshield wipers. God Bless Stormin' Norman.

Kenny Sez: "I don't think in inches, feet, yards, miles, meters, kilometers, or the like. My head tends to calculate in paddle, canoe, or kayak lengths. Ever since I had that bad spell of water in my ears"

1 hr. 18 min. in / 22 min. to go: BIG alcove sits to the left as the river bends right. On your approach to this alcove, it looks as though the river is coming to a T, and that perhaps you have reached an island around which the river flows both left and right. Stay to the right.

1 hr. 28 min. in / 12 min. to go: A Maple River rarity on water with so many long straight aways: the river flows in a horseshoe pattern to the left around the shore, creating today's first peninsula.

1 hour and 40 minutes in: 4 minutes after passing the first home seen today, we're at the Maple River Campground and the trip's end. Take out on the left.

THE TOWN: HUBBARDSTON

Detroit Tigers local radio affiliate: WVFN 730 AM (Lansing)

When you're out driving, and take the time to get off of the expressways, even staying away from the 2 lane state roads, and follow those little gray lines on the map known as county roads, the village of Hubbardston is the kind of quaint small town that is a happy surprise. Hubbardston sits along Fish Creek, a tributary of the Maple. The downtown park has a dam and a pond that makes for a scenic sitting location.

In the early 1800s, there were few inhabitants in what is now Hubbardston, only roaming nomadic tribes of Chippewa and Ottawa Indians. By the 1840s and 50s, Irish immigrants came in numbers, creating a large Irish settlement. About this time, a group of men that included Thomas Hubbard, for whom the town was named, purchased substantial tracts of pine along Fish Creek. His group started up what became a thriving lumber and grist mill operation. By 1868, 100 barrels per day of "Pride of the West" brand flour, touted as "second only in quality to the highest grades manufactured in St. Louis, Missouri" were being produced. The mill success, along with the demand for the area pines, made the village of Hubbardston quite prosperous by the 1870s. An example of the good times was in the wages paid by the lumber camps: $25 to $30 per month, and room & board to boot!

Hubbardston in the late-1800s was popular for something other that it's quality flour and seemingly endless pine trees: her famed mineral baths. Folks from all over Michigan came seeking the town's mineral bath healing waters, heavy with iron and sulfur, believed to be particularly good in treating rheumatism, and quite possibly "second only in quality to a jug of Granny Clampett's rheumatism medicine" (please note: this is only the author's assumption).

From a peak population of 1,200 and "more than a few saloons" in the mill and lumber heyday near the end of the 1800s, today Hubbardston is home to 400 residents and one single tavern, Shiels. The small number of businesses and the picturesque park give the town a very comfortable Mayberry feel.

Sources: "Hubbardston, Yesterday And Today" by Helen A. Cusack, Beverly Hillbillies

THE TAVERN: SHIELS TAVERN

Of Hubbardston's first Irish settlers, 9 of the families came from Tipperary. And, since it's a long way to, and from, Tipperary, the travel of such a distance can build a powerful thirst. So, it's appropriate that a very Irish tavern would serve the good folks of Hubbardston: Shiels Tavern.

A tavern sign asks you to "Enjoy yourself with good food, cold drinks and meet great friends". It's hard to find fault with such a sales pitch.

Shiels claims to be the oldest tavern in Michigan. Originally opened in the late-1800s, Shiels now holds the oldest liquor license issued in the state that remains under the same name. Prior to Prohibition, a license to sell liquor was not required. Terence E. Shiels obtained the bar's first liquor license in 1936, and every Shiels license since that first one in 1936 is posted behind glass on one of the tavern's walls.

The antique bar (an old classic!) and the back bar (<u>real</u> nice wooden frame) were brought to Shiels by horse and wagon from Fowler. It's a sweet bar for the regulars to belly up to.

Yes, Shiels is very, very Irish. Guinness in bottles… in the middle of the back bar mirror is a wooden sign counting down the days to St. Patty's… and a sign announcing, "Parking for Irish only – all others will be towed".

There is, however, room for multiculturalism at Shiels: it was our good fortune to be visiting during "Taco Tuesdays". 75 cent tacos from noon on, Taco Tuesdays feature tacos at a great value, generously sized with good flavor. Mister P says, "Taco Tuesdays is the only way to go!" Looking for something other than beef in your taco? Don't even go there. To Tommy's inquiries about fish and chicken options, waitress Kelly silently replied with a quizzical look which said all that needed to be said.

As the final multi-cultural confirmation, yes, Shiels does sell Pabst Blue Ribbon, always a sure sign of quality. In the adjacent side room, more than even the nice wood paneling and the darts, the finest feature is the very large PBR wall sign. Even a tavern this Irish can't deny Pabst Germanic goodness. A Gaelic toast then, to Jacob Best, founder of Pabst: "Slainte, Jacob!"

RIVER RAISIN
DUNDEE, MICHIGAN

RIVER SOUNDTRACK:
Rollin' & Tumblin' – Muddy Waters
Glad – Traffic
Rotten Egg – Gas Huffer
Story Of My Life – Unrelated Segments
Down By The River – Neil Young

CANOE LIVERY:
River Raisin Canoe Livery
owners Chuck & Cherry Haddix
1151 Plank Road, Dundee Mi 48131
The entrance to the livery is 10 miles east of
US23 on Plank Rd.
Phone (734) 529-9029
website www.riverraisincanoelivery.com

Raisin River

Level One
Beginner Ability Required

THE BACKGROUND: RIVER RAISIN

So this is what urban canoeing is like. It's busy. It's different. It's fun. We put in amidst the traffic of downtown Dundee, just to the east of the town's triangular town square, at the M50 Bridge. Just upstream & clearly visible from our launching point is the Dundee Dam. In terms of River Raisin water flow control, this is the most important dam on the river. The River Raisin flows 140 miles, from its headwaters near the town of Brooklyn (think Irish Hills & Michigan International Speedway), until it empties into Lake Erie at Monroe. The river is a slow meander and, at least on the stretch of the suggested trip, is murky and muddy-looking. French explorers, noting the wild grapes growing along the banks of the river, gave the river its name, as *raisin* is French for grape.

The Muddy Waters crew: Gilda Weaks with nieces Ashana Smith, LaDana Couch & nephew Darryl T Couch, Gus Weaks, birthday girl Madelynn Weaks, Gloria Weaks, Chris Weaks, Ronnie Jr. Swiecki, Tina Swiecki, Ron Swiecki, Andy Kocembo, Paul Brown, Maggie and me.

THE RIVER: PADDLING THE RAISIN

The suggested trip runs 2 hours and 35 minutes, with the put in at the M50 Bridge in downtown Dundee. There will be no campgrounds and no toilets on today's ride.

As we begin this stretch, the river is 70' wide and 1' deep. 5 minutes in, a fish jumps out of the water and into Gilda's lap. Its stay was brief and memorable. The fish was tossed back into the murky shallows by Chris, ending Gilda's involuntary participation in a catch 'n release program.

15 min. in / 2 hr. 20 min. to go: You float beneath a train trestle. The rocky, unkind slope to your right takes you to M50. At the top of the slope, turn left for a short walk to Thirsty's (see "The Tavern"). 2 minutes downstream from the train trestle, fun light rapids add some chop to the river, starting and ending within a minute.

Near the shore lies a partially submerged shopping cart. Andy declares it "a hobo canoe".

30 min. in / 2 hr. 5 min. to go: You are a half-hour into your Raisin adventure when, on the left shore, you pass an 80' tall river birch w/ 3 trunks. The river here has deepened to 3'.

45 min. in / 1 hr. 50 min. to go: Paddle below power lines.

1 hr. in / 1 hr. 35 min. to go: Preceded 120' by a fallen tree from the left shore, two stone islands, separated by 20' of open water, extend into the river from the left bank. The 2nd island, the larger of the two, stretches half-way across the water and offers plenty of room for a canoeing break. The river, squeezed by the islands, is choppy at the tip of island #2.

1 hr. 12 min. in / 1 hr. 23 min. to go: "Curve Left" yellow street sign sits high on the left shore tree. Disobey the sign, and you'll paddle into a lagoon as the river bends left.

1 hr. 20 min. in / 1 hr. 15 min. to go: Five majestic river birches line the left bank.

Kenny Sez: *"I plan to get to my chores once I'm off the river. There should be enough water in the Lower Peninsula alone to keep me away from work for two years."*

1 hr. 30 min. in / 1 hr. 5 min. to go: The fallen tree from the right shore blocks half of the river, creating light rapids for 100'. 2 minutes downstream, paddle beneath power lines where the river bends left. Also to the left sits a large home with a long, sloping lawn.

1 hr. 35 min. in / 1 hr. to go: 60 minutes remain in your trip when you reach the large island on the left. The island announces its presence on its upstream edge with a creek, 15' wide at its mouth, on your left. Stay to the right. Marking the downstream tip of the island is a creek 25' wide at its junction with the river.

1 hr. 40 min. in / 55 min. to go: P-U! Do NOT get out of your boat here! On the right shore as the river bends right is a nice looking beach, what appears to be today's best spot to pull the canoes over and stretch your legs. Don't do it! Every footstep on this beach releases naturally-occurring sulfur that smells like rotten eggs.

1 hr. 50 min. in / 45 min. to go: A 50'-long silver pipe leans down towards the river from the right bank. Balancing this man-made intrusion is the poetry of two blue herons. Sitting along the shore when we first approached, they took to the sky, disappearing from our view. Over the next 30 minutes, a neat routine would play itself out: our boats would round a bend, approaching the herons standing on the shore. The birds would rise slowly into the sky before we got too close, flying out of sight. We paddle around a bend, see the herons on shore. We get too close; they gracefully fly out of sight – until the next bend.

1 hr. 55 min. in / 40 min. to go: A fine looking creek enters the River Raisin from the left, 20' wide at its mouth.

2 hrs 10 min. in / 25 min. to go: Along the left shore sits a 150' long, unfinished seawall. 5 minutes downstream, you'll float below power lines, just before the river bends right.

2 hours and 35 minutes and you arrive at the take out point: the campground of the River Raisin Canoe Livery. Exit at the dock on the left.

THE TOWN: DUNDEE

Detroit Tigers local radio affiliate: WLQR 1470 AM (Toledo)

Scottish proverb #1: "He was a bold man who first ate a Haggis"

Perhaps Dundee's Cabela's – the only Michigan location of the sporting goods giant – should sell kilts along with their hunting, fishing, & outdoor gear. You see, there are two views of how Dundee got her name, both with Scottish origins. The first, and generally considered the most likely, is that the town was named after Dundee, Scotland.

Scottish proverb #2: "Never argue – simply keep repeating your assertion"

The more exciting view, although perhaps a bit less likely, is that the town was named after Bonnie Dundee. A Lord in the 1600s, Bonnie Dundee was not one to lie about the castle counting his silver & gold. Rather, he was a soldier of fortune, who conducted many chivalrous missions with dash and élan.

Scottish proverb #3: "Whiskey may not cure the common cold – but it fails more agreeably than most other things"

Bonnie Dundee became a Scottish hero for his courage in defeating the invaders at the Pass of Killiecrankie. Although he fell in the very moment of victory, his glorious actions & name live forever in Scottish lore… and maybe in a small town along the River Raisin.

Dundee, Michigan was established as a village in 1823. Settlement of this geographical area made sense: sitting as it does on a narrow bend on the River Raisin, it is the ideal location for placement of a road heading straight west from Monroe, a critical town in Territorial (pre-statehood) Michigan.

Henry Ford was directly involved with the town in the 1930s, through his efforts with the Old Mill, a landmark listed on the National Register of Historic Places. The Old Mill was built in 1850, and had been used since that time until 1925 first as a gristmill, and then in the early 1900s employed to generate electricity. In 1934, having been vacated for 10 years, the building was to be torn down. Henry Ford saw a new use for the structure: to be used to show folks how waterpower could better be used in rural areas. Over the two-year period of 1934 & 1935, while the Mickey Cochrane-led Detroit Tigers were winning back-to-back pennants and their 1st World Championship (excuse this dry land meander), Henry Ford restored the mill and, using limestone from the Raisin riverbed, built an addition to house a new turbine. Henry's new "village factory" (one of 20 Ford built on Southeast Michigan rivers between 1919 and 1944) was productive for the next twenty years as a manufacturing location for producing copper tips for welding machines. Today, the Old Mill serves Dundee as both a museum and as a community center. The building received its National Historic Place designation in 1990.
Sources: www.dundeevillage.net, www.wikipedia.org, www.fife.50megs.com

THE TAVERN: THIRSTY'S PUB & GRUB

Thirsty's Pub & Grub is located less than 1 mile east of Dundee along M50. "We like to think it's the Cheers of Dundee" the bar proclaims on its menu. While it's true that no Norm Peterson witticisms were overheard during our visit (example "How's a beer sound Norm?"; "I dunno. I usually finish 'em before they get a word in."), our group would endorse a stop at Thirsty's to anyone visiting or passing through Dundee.

Our extensive tavern research has not revealed a finer post-canoeing spot to unwind when it comes to a bite 'n a beer. Our table unanimously agreed that the pizza was excellent, with crust baked to perfection, and the burgers very good. The steak fries, usually not a favorite of a few of these Raisin swashbucklers, were by far the best we've ever had. And, just when you didn't think the meal could get any better, you find out that Thirsty's stocks Pabst Blue Ribbon longnecks - always a sure sign of quality.

If breakfast is what you seek at a tavern, you can order the "rise & shine" burger (how 'bout that Toni?) which includes bacon, cheese, and a fried egg. Thirsty's also features a Friday night fish fry, a pool table (with an overhead camera showing the table on a big screen), video games, a juke box, and enough TV screens to watch the day's main sporting event from anywhere you sit.

I don't know if it was the happy stupor that Thirsty's fare put me into or not, but maybe I did hear Norm Peterson's voice: "Whatcha up to Norm?"; "My ideal weight if I were eleven feet tall".

ROCKY RIVER
THREE RIVERS, MICHIGAN

RIVER SOUNDTRACK:
Fractured Fairy Tales (from Rocky & Bullwinkle)
Sun Arise – Alice Cooper
Man of Constant Sorrow – Soggy Bottom Boys
Hot Rod Lincoln – Commander Cody
Rivers of Babylon – The Melodians

CANOE LIVERY:
Liquid Therapy Canoe & Kayak Rentals
owners Ernie Manges and Karen McDonald
221 S. Main Street, Three Rivers MI 49093
Phone (269) 273-9000
www.liquidtherapypaddling.com

RIVER QUOTE:
Ernie Manges *"If you fall out of the boat… stand up."*

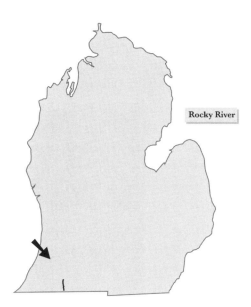

Rocky River

Level Two
Intermediate Ability Required

THE BACKGROUND: ROCKY RIVER

St. Joseph County has over 150 miles of navigable rivers. Karen and Ernie would like to get you out on to each and every one of those 150. Their canoe & kayak rental company, Liquid Therapy (how can you <u>not</u> love that name?), offers paddling adventures on six rivers: Rocky, Portage, Prairie, Fawn, Pigeon, and St. Joseph. The plan of our crack research team was to paddle the Prairie River. That was until I saw the beauty of the Rocky River while driving over it on the Michigan Avenue Bridge in the town of Three Rivers. The view looking north from the bridge is sweet: the Rocky white water flows beneath a foot bridge, cascading down over a series of rocks before wrapping around a grassy island. The white water continues below Michigan Avenue, ending moments downstream at its merger with the St. Joseph River.

Still debating whether to float the Rocky or the Prairie, and while waiting for the rest of the crack researchers to arrive for our day on the river, I stopped into a downtown Three Rivers restaurant. Grabbing a bite, I asked two locals about their rivers, and to see if they could direct me to a fine old time tavern for post-canoeing relaxation (an inquiry along the lines of a *Cash Cab* "shout out"). *"Oh, you fellas will want to go to Brewster's Tavern. You can't miss it – it's right on the Rocky River. In fact, you can pull your boat right up to it"*. Guess that the Prairie River will be in my next Michigan River book.

The Rocky Raconteur crack researchers: Kanoo Kenny Umphrey, his grandson Ethan Chandler Blake, and me.

THE RIVER: PADDLING THE ROCKY

The total time of the suggested trip is 2 hours and 25 minutes, launching from the Null Road Bridge. The river here is 35' wide and 4' deep (the depth today will range from 6" to 4'). The river floor is covered with tall reeds that, at times, create a blanket covering the river's surface. On the left shore are private homes. There are no toilets or parks along the journey.

10 min. in / 2 hrs 15 min. to go: The canoes float over the "rocking log". You'll know exactly what we're talking about when you approach it.

18 min. in / 2 hrs 7 min. to go: Seaweed is choking the Rocky's surface, forcing you to expend quite a bit of energy to paddle through it. There are times on this trip that, if you didn't paddle, you would come to a stop. While passing several homes on the right bank, and downstream from where the river bends left, a large log has fallen from the right. There is room to float by on the left.

River Bonus! Liquid Therapy canoes each come equipped with 3 insulated drink holders.

30 min. in / 1 hr. 55 min. to go: Separated by 20' are two fallen trees each from the right shore. As you pass the first tree on the far left, a tangle of branches from the left shore forces you to cut back quickly to your right, & then straighten the canoe to shoot the gap.

40 min. in / 1 hr. 45 min. to go: _Moon over the Rocky_. On the left bank, a huge uprooted tree has its bottom exposed, kind of mooning you as you paddle by. The tree bottom, perfectly perpendicular to the river bank, stands 15' tall.

50 min. in / 1 hr. 35 min. to go: Float beneath the Old Grass Bridge, with two of the biggest culverts

that you'll paddle through on a river. 5 minutes downstream, you paddle below another bridge. Another 5 minutes downstream, the first blue heron sighting today, at a small island just right of midstream. More blue herons will be seen today on the river.

1 hr. 10 min. in / 1 hr. 15 min. to go: The big island is the approximate half-way point of the trip. The easier passage is to the left, also the side you want to be on as you encounter the next island, immediately downstream. At this second island, a fallen tree completely blocks passage on the right. Deer are watching us from the shore, possibly wagering on how many silly humans will try to get through on the island's right. To the sound of deer laughter (throatier than you would think), I try right, can't get through, and have to back my canoe out.

At the end of the two islands, within a short stretch, are a large number of fallen trees to be maneuvered around, proving to be a fun exercise of paddling skills.

Kenny Sez: *"My 9-year old grandson wants to move to Michigan. He thinks that the whole state is a river and that everyone canoes all day long."*

1 hr. 40 min. in / 45 min. to go: *Double Moons over the Rocky.* 20' apart on the left bank are two uprooted trees, bottoms up facing us, perpendicular to the river's edge.

1 hr. 45 min. in / 40 min. to go: Float beneath US131. Five minutes downstream, and on our left, it's… a Bar on the River! The locals weren't just having fun with us. The bar, "Brewster's", sits just a few feet off of the left bank, within sight of the Hoffman Road Bridge a bit further downstream. See *"The Tavern"* section for a Brewster's description.

2 minutes after getting back into our canoes, we float below the Hoffman Road Bridge.

1 hr. 55 min. in / 30 min. to go: Back-to-back islands are left of midstream, passable either right or left. The main body of the river at 40' wide is on the right, while water on the left is 15' wide. We encounter some bottom-skimming.

2 hrs 10 min. in / 15 min. to go: As you float below a large bridge, you encounter a rocky waterfall, providing a fun 25' long run. There are slightly less rocks if you stay far right. Immediately

downstream is a large island where the right passage is very shallow (ducks appeared to be walking on the river surface!), so we passed on the left.

2 hrs 15 min. in / 10 min. to go: Float beneath a red wooden footbridge as you paddle around the left side of a big island.

Strongly Suggested Portage: Just beyond the tip of this island, following the river's main body to the left, you enter an extremely tricky, rocky, and dangerous mini-waterfall (part of the sweet scenery viewed from the Michigan Ave. Bridge – beautiful, but dangerous). This can be avoided by a portage that's accessible by paddling to the right and beyond the tall, wild grass. Exit here and walk your boat to just beyond the waterfall at the edge of the wooden sidewalk. *Note*: Ernie told us that in the year of our trip, 12 canoes tried to run this stretch, and only one made it through without tipping (falling into these rocks would not be pleasant). Kayaks were a bit more successful, but only a bit.

5 minutes remain after the portage. As you float beneath Michigan Avenue, and along side scenic Scidmore Park, several challenging white water runs are ahead, all very fun to run! Once the white water subsides, the Rocky River ends at its merger with the St. Joseph River, the very wide body of water on the left. Paddle across the St. Joe to the Liquid Therapy ramp on the left shore.

THE TOWN: THREE RIVERS

Detroit Tigers local radio affiliate: WMSH 1230 AM (Sturgis)

Three Rivers is located midway between Detroit and Chicago. A visit to the town would make a great weekend getaway. Besides enjoying the natural beauty of its waterways, a walk through its central business district is a treat – many of the older building facades have been restored, and are fascinating sights. Three Rivers downtown is listed in the National Register of Historic Places, due in large part to the significant number of well-preserved buildings of Victorian design.

"Nothing Lives Long – Except the Earth, the Mountains, the River"

The town of Three Rivers is so named as it is the location where the Rocky and Portage Rivers merge with the St. Joseph River. The confluence of the 3 waterways made this a favorite camping site for Native Americans for hundreds of years before being discovered by European settlers. LaSalle saw the natural beauty of the area on his 1680 travels, and the word was soon out, bringing many Frenchmen in his wake. In the 200 years prior to this, the Potawatomi Indians hunted the land, fished the rivers, and roamed the prairies. The Potawatomi nation stretched from southern Michigan to northern Indiana. Under the heading of symmetry (Three Rivers/Three Tribes), the Potawatomi were closely related to the Ottawa and Chippewa tribes, forming a loose federation known as the "Brothers of Three Fires".

Potawatomi Chief Cush-ee-wees: "We have so little, they have so much… Why do they want ours?"

Since LaSalle's 1680 visit, the Indians watched the intrusion of their land by explorers, missionaries, trappers, traders, and soldiers. The 1821 Chicago Treaty, signed by Gov. Cass and tribal chiefs, sold most Potawatomi land to the U.S. government, leaving the Indians only scattered reservations. When a subsequent treaty tricked the tribe into selling these few reservations, many Potawatomi would not honor this treaty, and refused to leave the land. In 1840, the U.S. Army used force to round up the Indians and move them west of the Mississippi. Some Indians hid in the forest until the soldiers had gone, but they had no home to return to.

Three Rivers was founded in 1830. The town was as far as large boats could come up the St. Joseph River. From here, flatboats and rafts were used to carry goods to and from Lake Michigan. George Buck, Jr., came to Three Rivers with his parents in 1830: "There were three camps of Indians near by. They came to our house quite often to hold Indian dances. They would gather, dance all night, and in the morning go about their business. We never locked our house. The latch string was always out. The Indians were in the habit of coming in at night, sitting around the fire, chatting and smoking and when they got ready to sleep they would roll up their blankets on the floor and by day light would be gone."

Mrs. Sophia Salsig, daughter of pioneer Jacob McInterfer: "The Indians were very friendly as they had a good chief, Sag-e-naw. He died in 1831 and was buried down near Hog Creek (Prairie River)… We all went and gave the Chief a decent burial… There was no underbrush, and the woods were beautiful just like a flower garden."

Sources: Michigan Historic Site markers," Three Rivers, The Early Years" by Lucile Haring & Phyllis Agosti

THE TAVERN: BREWSTER'S

A bar sitting right alongside the river that you can paddle up to. As a canoer or kayaker, can there be a better location? Brewster's can be floated to 5 minutes downstream from the US131 Bridge, a short walk up the grassy slope from the left shore. There is plenty of outdoor seating on the big deck overlooking the river, but the comfortable feel inside could lure you in for a spell.

The adjective for Brewster's pizza would be scrumptious! Their menu ranges far and wide, and includes nachos, salmon, walleye, swordfish, and - if after lunch you'd like to nap on the grassy slope before continuing to float downstream - there's the Titan Burger, as big a meal as it sounds.

Walking indoors, the dining area is to the left, and a bar you could homestead in all day is on the right. Although you're right at home without this, the bar has 7 TVs, about one per bar stool… and the 6 booths in the dining area each have their own TV. Brewster's TV fixation reminds one of the "Taxi" episode in which Jim Ignatowski got his act together, worked hard, made a lot of money, and spent it all on… a wall of TVs.

Brewster's does have one character flaw: they do not serve Pabst Blue Ribbon. One was able to get past this by repeating over and over the mantra, "They're right on the river. They're right on the river. They're right on the river."

How many bottles of Pabst could you buy for the price of 13 TVs?

ROGUE RIVER
ROCKFORD, MICHIGAN

CANOE LIVERY:
Powers Outdoors
owners Greg & Jake Slominski,
65 Main Street, Rockford, Mi 49341
Phone (616) 863-8107,
www.powersoutdoors.com

RIVER QUOTE:
Tommy, "Take me down by the rock pile, honey. I'm a little boulder there."

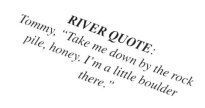

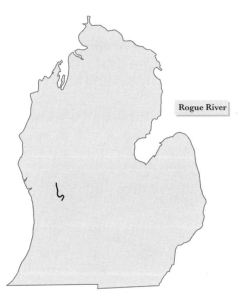

Rogue River

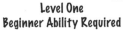

Level One
Beginner Ability Required

THE BACKGROUND: ROGUE RIVER

The Rogue River was meant to have a different name. In the 1830s, a survey team was doing their work in the wilderness area that is now Rockford. One member of the team was from the Detroit area. He wished to honor his hometown, and decided to name the wilderness area river after the big river in Detroit – the Rouge River. However, the surveyor misspelled Rouge in his notes, flipping the "u" with the "g". By the time his error was discovered, the name Rogue had become commonly used among other surveyors, and a fait accompli.

The Rogue was formed as an outlet to a glacial lake – eventually named Rice Lake - in southeastern Newaygo County. Over the years, Rice Lake shrank first to a pond and, by the early-1900s, was completely drained into the Rogue River. The streams and springs that formerly fed Rice Lake are now the headwaters of the Rogue. From Newaygo, the Rogue flows south & east for 35 miles until its eventual junction with the Grand River just north of Grand Rapids. For thousands of years before the Europeans arrived, the Rogue was the main transportation route linking Native Americans in the Grand Rapids area with their cousins near Newaygo. In 1683, French explorer De La Salle, while on an expedition of the Grand River, was believed to be the first white man to see the Rogue.

The Rogue research team: Perry "Klink" VerMerris, Tom-quamenon Holbrook, & Doc.

THE RIVER: PADDLING THE ROGUE

The suggested float down the Rogue runs approximately 2 hours. There are no DNR or Forest Service authorized camping areas along the way, nor are there any toilets. Trip details were noted during a mid-September paddle, when water levels are below normal.

The put in point is at 12 Mile Road Bridge at Friske Road. The river depth as you begin is 2' to 3' and the river width is 30' across. Trees leaning in from both banks create a natural canopy over much of the river, while a great deal of sun finds its way through breaks in the canopy. Good looking homes are seen along the right shore.

Brook trout, rainbow trout, and steelhead are caught in healthy quantities in the Rogue.

15 min. in / 1 hr. 52 min. to go: As the river bends left, near a home on the right shore, 150' of fun light rapids runs through a rock garden. A blue heron flies just ahead.

25 min. in / 1 hr. 42 min. to go: Passing the little island is blocked on the right by a fallen tree and other debris. There's a nice, little white water run as you pass on the left.

37 min. in / 1 hr. 30 min. to go: You float beneath the US131 Bridge and its southbound lanes. There's nice wildlife scenery just downstream from the bridge: several friendly ducks float alongside the boats, and a raccoon rebelling against the nocturnal lifestyle hangs out on the right bank.

42 min. in / 1 hr. 25 min. to go: Drift below the US131 Bridge and its northbound lanes.

This river is too cool. Throughout the trip, sunlight dances on the frequent light white water runs, while trees along the riverside gently bow down towards the water. Quite a few comments to get back here <u>soon</u> were made barely 20 minutes into the trip.

51 min. in / 1 hr. 16 min. to go: From the left, a pretty little creek, christened "Leak Creek", merges with the Rogue. 50' up the creek, the current does a limbo under a fallen tree that stretches from bank to bank.

56 min. in / 1 hr. 11 min. to go: 200' of very light rapids as the river bends left

1 hr. 10 min. in / 57 min. to go: Float beneath 12 Mile Road Bridge. An island lies just a few feet downstream. Whether you pass on the right or the left, you'll experience a great light rapids run – very fun!

Kenny Sez: "The stages of my life are child, adult, and flood."

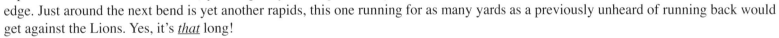

The river soon widens to 80' and shallows to 6", but with no bottom scraping.

1 hr. 32 min. in / 35 min. to go: On the left high bank sits a small wooden viewing deck, a part of the 92-mile long White Pine Trail. Directly across the river, the bank is pullover-and-take-a-break friendly, with plenty of flat ground beyond the river's edge. Just around the next bend is yet another rapids, this one running for as many yards as a previously unheard of running back would get against the Lions. Yes, it's *that* long!

The Rogue is dotted sporadically with large rocks that stick their heads 1 or 2 feet above the river's surface. The river floor is sandy with occasional pebbles (the only Flintstone known to be on the Rogue).

1 hr. 37 min. in / 30 min. to go: You know that there's one half hour left in the trip when you see the couple hundred foot long stone seawall on your right. The seawall fronts the home with the long stairway to the river.

1 hr. 50 min. in / 17 min. to go: On the river's right, it's suddenly very marshy. A creek or long lagoon sits to the right of the tall reeds. Several homes are beyond those reeds. The river is soon deeper than the length of your paddle.

The Rogue River Spreads

1 hr. 52 min. in / 15 min. to go: Hard right is a 10' wide channel that very suddenly tells you that you've come upon an island. Taking this 10' wide channel is the more direct route downstream, even as the main body of the Rogue flows left. This break in the river heralds the start of the Rogue River Spreads, which runs for the next 8 minutes. These spreads are much more sprawling and wider bank-to-bank than

those spreads found on either the Fox River or the White River. Within the spreads, you encounter multiple islands and, whether you pass each one right or left, you'll then encounter additional islands. Any route paddled will be the right one, and all routes taken come back to one uninterrupted body of water. Swans, turtles, & Canadian Geese are just a few feet away. On the left shore, bicyclers on the White Pine Trail come clearly into view.

2 hrs in / 7 min. to go: As the spreads come to an end, the river shallows to 2' deep. To your left are the cream-colored buildings of Wolverine World Wide, makers of Hush Puppies brand shoes. A long-running wooden walkway is high above on the right bank.

2 hours, 7 minutes and you're in! Take out on the left, 100' before the Rockford Dam.

THE TOWN: ROCKFORD

Detroit Tigers local radio affiliate: WLAV 97.1FM & WBBL 1340AM (Grand Rapids).

Love that basset hound! Rockford is home to the world-famous (sold in over 120 countries) Hush Puppies brand shoes. Hush Puppies parent company – and Rockford's largest employer – is Wolverine World Wide, who also makes shoes & boots under the Harley-Davidson, Caterpillar, Patagonia, & Stanley brand labels.

Rockford's founder is a man by the name of Smith Lapham. Hired in 1843 to complete the first Rogue sawmill and dam, with a promised reward of 80 acres riverside, Smith instead received a reduced payment of 40 acres. Rather than fuss about this, Smith built his own sawmill, apparently a very good one, as the mill of the man who short-changed Lapham was soon closed & that fellow soon forgotten. Smith and his sawmill prospered. At this time, Illinois & Iowa were being heavily settled. Fertile but treeless, settlement of these areas created a big demand for Michigan's white pine lumber. Opportunities for employment at the sawmill took off, these new workers built homes along the Rogue, and the town of Rockford (known as "Laphamville" from 1845 to 1865) was established.

In 1867, the 1st trains to Rockford began running on the Grand Rapids & Indiana Railroad Line. In 1994, through the "rails to trails" program, this riverside rail line was transformed into the White Pine Trail, running 92 miles from Riverside Park in Grand Rapids in the south to Cadillac in the north, a wonderful place for walkers, runners, bikers, & rollerbladers.

At the end of a great day exploring Rockford (supplemental land-based research courtesy Mister P, Toni, and Maggie), Frenz Coffeehouse schedules some fine music (catch the Michigan-based *Squeaky Clean Cretins* when you can), before turning in for the night at Grandma's Bed & Breakfast. Chi Chi and Larry have owned and run Grandma's since before you were born. A wonderful couple, our hosts were interesting breakfast companions: Chi Chi previously served as mayor of Rockford and, when not running her B&B, can be seen greeting folks at the local Meijer.

Sources: "From Sawmill to City" by Homer L. Burch, Rockford Living Magazine

THE TAVERNS: ROGUE RIVER TAVERN & GRILL ONE ELEVEN

The Rogue River Tavern is a fine spot to kick back at after a Rogue float. The staff that we encountered was friendly, apologizing for the absence of Pabst Blue Ribbons on their menu. The room on the left is where you belly up to the bar with a basket of chips and a cold one. The room on the right is a spacious one with two pool tables, 3 video machines, and a digital juke box. This room has a big ole dance floor for Saturday night jumpin' up and down to classic rock or country bands.

Grill One Eleven is upscale but comfortable. We enjoyed sitting upstairs on their back deck for some excellent food and Pabst longnecks (which, of course, always goes well with excellent food). During the summer months, the back deck windows come off for open air enjoyment. Our waitress Megan was a real treat, introducing us to Pabst-mimosas (surprisingly good! who knew?). Right next door, run by the same owners, is Marinades Pizza Bistro – their wood-fired pizza is excellent.

ROUGE RIVER DETROIT, MICHIGAN

RIVER SOUNDTRACK:
See Emily Play – Polka Floyd
Little By Little – Junior Wells
Limbo Rock – Chubby Checker
Room To Move – John Mayall
1969 – the Stooges,
Reach Out, I'll Be There – the Four Tops
(Levi Stubbs tribute)

CANOE LIVERY:
Heavner Canoe Rental
owner Al Heavner
2775 Garden Road, Milford MI 48381
Phone (248) 685-2379
www.heavnercanoe.com
*(note: Heavner's primarily services the Huron River, but
also services any river without a local livery)*

RIVER QUOTE:
*Chris (Detroit native), "The Rouge is
too thick to drink, too thin to plow."*

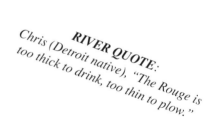

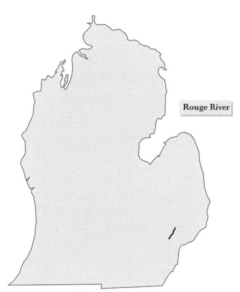

Rouge River

Level Two
Intermediate Ability Required

THE BACKGROUND: ROUGE RIVER

1967 Detroit catches fire. 1968 the Tigers catch fire. 1969 the Rouge catches fire. Which event was more impressive is open to debate.

The Rouge runs for 126 miles until its rendezvous with the Detroit River. The river is made up of 4 branches: the main with headwaters in SW Rochester Hills, the upper with headwaters in NE Novi, the middle with headwaters in Northville, and the lower with headwaters in Washtenaw County's Superior Township.

Growing up in Detroit, the Rouge was our river… the river. The perfect river for Detroit: historic, princely in its heyday, badly abused by polluters, resilient, its recovery a work in progress. At its lowest point, from when it caught fire in 1969 to the mid-1980s, the Rouge was believed to be one of the country's most polluted rivers due in large part to long term dumping of both industrial waste and untreated sewage into the Rouge.

The fortunes of the river turned in 1986 with the formation of the Friends of the Rouge, the same year that the Friends conducted their first annual Rouge Rescue river clean-up.

20+ years of Rouge Rescues have resulted in 30,000 folks removing tons of trash and fallen trees from the river, 25,000 students & adults monitoring the Rouge water quality, and workshops held to educate riverside (& other) residents regarding practices they can use at home to improve the health of the Rouge. The Friends of the Rouge also work with local governments to enact river clean-up projects in each shoreline community.

As of this writing, there are no canoe liveries along the Rouge. Enter Heavner's Canoe Rental. Owner Al Heavner has a passion to share his love of the outdoors with as many people as possible, and has shown a willingness to transport his canoes and kayaks from long distances, at a fair price, in order to put people on a river where no livery exist. Al's Milford office and satellite locations support and conduct classes and events throughout the state, at schools, churches, corporations, and any other entity that wishes to expand their knowledge of the outdoors. Heavner's "No Child Left Inside" program is designed to provide every child with a positive outdoor experience.

Sources: Friends of the Rouge, www.therouge.org, Wikipedia, Al Heavner

The Rouge Riparians, including many Friends of the Rouge: Sally Petrella, Paul Stark, Kurt Kuban, Bill Craig, Al VanKerckhove, Cyndi Ross, Sarah VanBuren, Betsy Nightingale, Sue Thompson, Christel Baloczki, Vicki Schroeder, Ken Sarkozy, Jason Brown, James Brown, Lou Szakal, Phyllis Kennedy, Luna Calley, Emily "Sweet 21" Cooper, Maggie and me.

A 5 minute video from the trip, produced by Paul Stark, can be seen on You Tube under "Canoe Trip on the Rouge River Oct. 25, 2008".

THE RIVER: PADDLING THE ROUGE

The suggested trip is on the Lower Branch of the Rouge, running for 1 hour and 25 minutes, including a 15 minute portage. As clean up efforts continue, and as more and more paddlers take to its waters, additional and longer Rouge floats will be available.

Our launch point was in Wayne at Goudy Park, located less than 1/10th of a mile north of Michigan Avenue on Wayne Road. We found that the best river entry point was just upstream from the big deck at the water's edge. There are no restrooms on this stretch.

At the put in, the river is running 20' wide and 2' deep, with a great deal of rocks on the river floor. Here bottom-skimming occurs. Within 50' of the launch is a brief rapids run, flowing over a rock ledge. Pass this on the left. A few feet downstream as you pass under the bridge, the water level is low enough to bring your boat to a halt unless you stay in the deeper water on the left.

Trees lean in from both the left and the right shores, creating a river portico for you to float beneath. The scenery is very Up North, with sparse signs that you're floating through a city.

25 min. in / 60 min. to go: Let's channel Chubby Checkers, "Time to limbo, mon. How low can you go?" A large fallen tree, leaning in from your right, lies across the river. Room to paddle below is on the left. 30' downstream, a tree fallen from the left bank is passable on your right. There's just enough space to limbo below both.

We paddled next to Friends of the Rouge Dan. As he was picking up some empties from the river he said, "Thank God for the bottle bill. That way I can at least pay for my gas on these Rouge trips".

34 min. in / 51 min. to go: Just over one-half hour in is a good-sized island on your right.

It's found just beyond an S curve in the Rouge that wraps around a series of nature's river obstacles. The obvious passage around the island is to your left.

40 min. in / 45 min. to go: You're almost half-way at the large fallen tree that must be floated under far right.

48 min. in / 37 min. to go: Big, dry and deep crevice cuts through the land on your right, working its way to the right bank.

Kenny Sez: "The river is the cure for the common day."

50 min. in / 35 min. to go: Separated by 50' are two fallen trees, both stretching from high bank to high bank, well above the water line. There's easy passage below each.

55 min. in / 30 min. to go: Float beneath the Venoy Road Bridge.

1 hr. 4 min. in / 21 min. to go: This is a big-time logjam, probably a good 50' or so deep. There's no head of steam forceful enough to plow your boat through this mass of tangle. 15 minutes of our remaining 21 minutes was spent getting our flotilla through here. Portage on the right.

1 hour and 25 minutes on the Rouge, and you're in. The Lower Rouge Parkway and exit from the river will be on your left.

THE TOWN: DETROIT

Detroit Tigers local radio affiliate: WXYT 1270 AM & 97.1 FM (Detroit).

French nobleman Antoine de la Mothe Cadillac established a trading post on the Detroit River in 1701. This settlement was first named Fort Pontchartrain, later renamed LaVille d'Etroit. In 1752, Cadillac's old trading post experienced one last name change, to Detroit. Detroit, a city that is historic, dynamic, and known in the 1920s as the "Paris of America". A city with a history that inspires. Imagine a day in 1919, 3 chairs pulled up on the banks of the Rouge, 1 each for Thomas Edison, Henry Ford, and Harvey Firestone.

Detroit, a city of firsts. In 1847, first English-speaking territory to ban capital punishment (due to citizen repulsion at the hanging of an innocent man). 1849, nation's first state fair. 1866, Vernor's Ginger Ale is created as the nation's first soda pop. 1876, first ice cream soda (thank you Fred Saunders). 1877, first telephone company. 1879, Detroit telephone customers become the first in the nation to be assigned phone numbers. 1880, first international telephone line (Detroit-Windsor). 1908, the Model T is introduced, the first car built on a moving assembly line, generally considered the first affordable car, the car that "put America on wheels". 1909, first concrete road, Woodward between 6 Mile and 7 Mile. 1920, first 4-way traffic light installed, at the corner of Woodward and Michigan Avenue. 1939, first air-conditioned car, built by the Packard Motor Car Company. 1941, Davidson Freeway is the nation's first expressway. 1954, Northland is America's first shopping mall.

The Sporting News picked Detroit as the number one sports town in America, and past successes have lifted the town's spirit when it was needed the most: in 1935, Detroit was known as the "City of Champions" when the Tigers, Red Wings, and the Lions reigned supreme, and the effect on the town's Depression-era mood was hard to overestimate. The 1968 World Series victory of the Tigers helped the city heal from the 1967 riots.

Detroit is Greektown and Motown, Henry Ford, the Finney House Barn (underground railroad), Ralph Bunche (diplomat, mediator, 1950 Nobel Prize Winner), Iggy and the Stooges, Francis Ford Coppola (filmmaker including "the Godfather"), Stroh Brewery, Charles Lindbergh, Bill "Rock Around the Clock" Haley, the White Stripes, William Burt (inventor of the solar compass and the typewriter), Bob Seger, Augustus Woodward (created plan for Detroit after the 1805 fire), Chief Pontiac, Jimmy Hoffa, Tiger Stadium, Hoot Robinson's, Prince Hal Newhouser, David Buick, Levi Stubbs, Bill Kennedy, J.P. McCarthy, Ed McMahon, the Black Bottom neighborhood and Paradise Valley (the rare 1930's nightspot where folks of different color enjoyed music side-by-side), Kid Rock, Gordie, Willie Horton, Tyrus Raymond Cobb, Bobby Layne, Joe Louis, and Bill Bonds challenging Mayor Coleman Young to a fist fight on local TV.

One of Detroit's finest is often forgotten: Hazen Pingree. A statue commemorating Hazen as "The Idol of The People" is located at Grand Circus Park. In 1889, Democrats ran the city, and business leaders nominated Pingree as the Republican challenger. Hazen was a man of means and, once elected, his rich supporters assumed that he would support policies favoring the well-to-do over the general populace. They were in for a rude awakening. Hazen championed the working man, instituting social reforms to benefit all. During the 1890s Depression, "Pingree's potato patches" sprung up all over Detroit, putting to work the unemployed creating gardens on vacant land, producing food to feed those in need (a program duplicated in other countries during hard times). He pioneered work relief programs, the first mayor to do so. When gas and light prices rose beyond the means of the average Detroit wage earner, he took control from private utilities and gave that control to the city. Previously, labor strikes were broken by the state militia – under Pingree, arbitration was used to solve such issues. Hazen Pingree was wildly popular with the people: elected mayor of Detroit twice and governor of Michigan four times. For a short time, he held both positions simultaneously, until the state Supreme Court ruled against this situation. Hazen is rated by historians as one of the top 10 mayors in United States history. As governor, he took on the railroads, pushing legislation forcing the railroads to pay equitable taxes. Although the railroads controlled 19 of the 32 members of the Michigan Senate, state residents' vocal support of the measure helped to push it through. In 1901, at age 60 and while still in office, Pingree arrived in London, fresh off of an African Safari with then U.S. Vice-President Theodore Roosevelt. On safari, Hazen was stricken with peritonitis, and died before he could make it home from London. Over 20,000 lined Woodward Avenue to pay their respects during his funeral procession.

Sources: Michigan history on line, Wikipedia, On-The-Road Histories

THE TAVERN: MILLER'S BAR – DEARBORN

"Where lesser burgers come to worship", announces the sign behind the bar. Located between our Rouge River launch point in Wayne and the City of Detroit, sits Miller's Bar on Michigan Ave., just east of Telegraph. The silly question of "may I have a menu?" was answered with "No menu. Burgers, burgers, burgers" (think Saturday Night Live and Belushi's "chee-burger, chee-burger"). Hmm, maybe I'll have a burger then. GQ Magazine, while listing the 20 best burgers in America, ranked Miller's #8. There's no pool table, or darts, etc. If you're coming to Miller's, you're coming to eat (burgers it is) and drink (Pabst Longnecks are offered – always a sure sign of quality!).

Combining Miller's old tyme charm with it's primarily business crowd, one gets the feeling that they're on the set of A&E's "Mad Men". Oh yes, and about those burgers… they <u>were</u> very good.

THORNAPPLE RIVER
HASTINGS, MICHIGAN

RIVER QUOTE:
Maggie, "The absence of lightening is appreciated"

RIVER SOUNDTRACK:
Singin' in the Rain – Gene Kelly
Time Machine – Grand Funk Railroad
William Tell Overture-Abridged – Walter Carlos
Candy Man – Mississippi John Hurt
Come As You Are – Nirvana

CANOE LIVERY:
U-Rent-Em Canoe Livery
owners Mike & Julie Fox
805 W. Apple St., Hastings MI 49058.
Phone (269) 945-3191
www.urentemcanoe.com

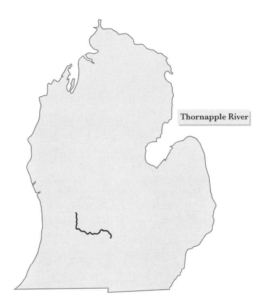

Thornapple River

Level One
Beginner Ability Required

THE BACKGROUND: THORNAPPLE RIVER

Long before the Europeans found our shores, Native Americans used canoeing as a main mode of transportation and, as it is for us today, a source of happy solitude. Local author & historian Esther Walton directed me to the Charlton Park Exhibit Hall, a few miles east of Hastings. On display at the Exhibition Hall are authentic Native American canoes. Guide Keith Murphy told us that some of these were recovered from the bottom of the Thornapple River. The canoes were likely used over 200 years ago, and are worth a visit.

The Thornapple River has its origins in Eaton County, southwest of Lansing, and is a major tributary of the Grand River. The Thornapple flows for 100 miles until it finally merges with the Grand River in Kent County. The river has a national reputation as a fine smallmouth bass stream. The suggested river trip is right in the middle of some of the river's best fishing, which runs from Nashville to the junction with the Coldwater River, north of Hastings.

Sources: www.trails.com, Wikipedia, Esther Walton, Keith Murphy

The Thornapple River rain-soaked Crack Researchers: Joanne Gibson, Pat Marten, Rick Ester, Perry VerMerris, Jeff Cripe, Tommy Holbrook, Maggie and me.

THE RIVER: PADDLING THE THORNAPPLE

Suggested trip runs 3 hours and 5 minutes, launching just downstream from the Charlton Park Bridge, near the Redneck Yacht Club, at the Rivergate Campground. Livery man Vern dropped us off and told us what to expect on the river. Please note that this trip was taken late in the season, on August 22, and that the river was running lower than average.

Restrooms are found at 3 locations: 35 minutes into the float at the McKeowen Road Bridge Park, 2 hours 20 minutes in at the "Hastings Riverwalk" access, and at Tyden Park 8 minutes from the trip's end.

As the trip begins, the river is running 120' across and 15' deep.

20 min. in / 2 hrs 45 min. to go: Merging from our left is a fair-sized creek. A fallen log a few feet up the creek blocks exploration attempts by our kayak team of Joanne and Pat. In just 20 minutes since the launch, the river depth has decreased from 15' to as shallow as a half-foot deep in some spots. The river is now 80' across.

30 min. in / 2 hrs 35 min. to go: In case anyone is in need of a break, but doesn't want to paddle to shore, sitting in the middle of the river is a picnic table, with seating for 8. There is a good deal of bottom-skimming over the next 10 minutes.

35 min. in / 2 hrs 30 min. to go: 120' apart, you float beneath two bridges. The first is the historic (built in 1903) McKeowen Road Bridge, now a pedestrian bridge, followed downstream by its modern vehicle replacement bridge. On the right bank, a beautiful park with restrooms has been created around the historic bridge. Two hawks are spotted.

43 min. in / 2 hrs 22 min. to go: Island populated with 50' tall trees is midstream. Slightly deeper water makes passing easier on the island's right. 1 minute beyond, a tree fallen from the right looks from a distance like it will be difficult to pass, but as you approach you see room to maneuver around on the tree's left. The tree marks the upstream edge of another island. The downstream tip of this island will be cleared in 3 minutes.

48 min. in / 2 hrs 17 min. to go: A tiny creek merges from the left. We see raccoons and two blue herons. There is plenty of trout among the reeds. A fisherman on shore is having a good day catching smallmouth bass.

1 hour in / 2 hrs 5 minutes to go: Paddle below the East River Road Bridge. The water is 3' deep and 60' wide.

1 hr. 22 min. in / 1 hr. 43 min. to go: On the left shore is a home with a nice park bench at the river's edge. 3 minutes downstream, where a creek rolls in from your right, an access friendly slope makes for a nice break spot to pull the boats over at.

Kenny Sez: *"A day down the river is a week of happiness."*

1 hr. 35 min. in / 1 hr. 30 min. to go: At the approximate half-way point of the journey begins a series of islands. Just downstream, the rocks along the shore are up to 3' in diameter, many sitting on the river floor next to clam shells and 1' tall reeds. There are many of these reeds on the back half of the trip, at times covering enough of the water's surface to create some drag on the bottom of canoes and kayaks.

2 hrs 5 min. in / 1 hour to go: You've reached the East Center Road Bridge. 7 minutes downstream, just past a dead creek on your left, a "Hastings City Limits" sign is visible beyond the homes on the left shore.

2 hrs 20 min. in / 45 min. to go: "Hastings Riverwalk" access point is on the left. At the river's edge is a deck with two park benches (a fine picnic location). A pavilion and restrooms are a short walk away. A walkway runs along the river's edge from this access spot to the trip's end at Apple Street, dotted with occasional small decks each with two park benches.

2 hrs 28 min. in / 37 min. to go: Meet up with a big island that takes 4 minutes to paddle past. The river's main flow at 60' wide is to the island's left, the water runs 25' wide on the island's right. 10 minutes from the end of this big island, you encounter a series of islands that are most easily passed on the left, due to shallow water on the right.

2 hrs 46 min. in / 19 min. to go: Float beneath 3 bridges over the next 9-10 minutes. East Mill Street Bridge is the old bridge with log supports. 4 minutes downstream, and you're at the Michigan Avenue Bridge. 5 minutes later and it's the Broadway Road Bridge and the eastern edge of Tyden Park.

Tyden Park is a large park with a pavilion, restrooms, and tennis courts. On a tall, granite pedestal is the statue of a Civil War soldier at parade rest, created in 1889. The statue inscription reads: *Dedicated to those who offered up their lives that the government of the people, by the people, and for the people, should not perish from the earth. To our nation's defenders, 1861-1865. The Union one and inseparable. Gettysburg. Vicksburg. Mission Ridge. Wilderness.*

3 hours and 5 minutes and you're in. Exit left at the U-Rent-Em Canoe trailer.

THE TOWN: HASTINGS

Detroit Tigers local radio affiliate: WLAV 96.9 FM & WBBL 1340 AM (Grand Rapids).

Hastings, rich in spring-fed lakes, and with a heavily-wooded and hilly countryside, has been referred to as "the only northern county in southern Michigan". The town is 40 miles southeast of Grand Rapids and 75 miles inland from Lake Michigan. Hastings was created in 1836 from 480 acres on the banks of the Thornapple River, property owned by Detroit banker Eurotas P. Hastings. Designated the county seat of Barry County in 1843, Today Hastings is vibrant enough, and rich enough in natural assets, to have been named "one of the 100 Best Small Towns in America" in a book by Norman Crampton.

One of Hastings most fascinating residents is Esther Walton, a member of the local historical society, who has also served the town as a contributing columnist to *The Hastings Banner* through her column "From Time To Time…". Esther's columns provide a unique look at Hastings from pre-pioneer days right up until today.

Before Hastings was settled, Barry County was the winter gathering place for some of the Indians who summered at the Straits of Mackinac, including the Ottawas, the Chippewas, and the Potawatomi. The Indian population grew from 30 families in the summer to 200 in the winter. They occupied wigwams made of poles covered with bark, cloth, and skins. The forests were their great parks, where they burned away underbrush so game would be visible from long distances. The rivers were their great highways, allowing migration to where food was most plentiful. These migrations were made in pirogues ("pee-ros") or dug-out canoes, or large birch bark boats. The dugouts were made with great labor from whitewoods logs. They were very narrow, and one inexperienced in handling them would likely be capsized. The silver birches needed to build birch bark canoes were scarce near Hastings, requiring a trip north for the needed trees. The birch barks were built from strips of bark sewed together with spruce root, & made water-tight with pitch (often pine rosin and animal fat). While floating downstream, the squaw paddled while her husband stood on the bow with a two-tined spear waiting for the fish.

There was a thin network of trails in Barry County. One of them, called the "Canada Trail" (near Charlton Park, just east of Hastings), was used by the warriors when they visited as far away as Fort Pontchartrain (Detroit) or crossed the Detroit River to visit tribesmen in Canada. Another, traversing the western part of the county and running north and south, connected the village of Match-eben-ashe-wish, today's Kalamazoo, with the village at the Rapids of the Grand, now Grand Rapids.

In connection with the waterways, these and other trails formed a complete system of communication. The Indians covered as much of their journey as they could by water. When water was not available for a trip or portion of a trip, they would draw their canoes up on shore and hide them so skillfully in either hollowed logs or with shrubbery that discovery was difficult. Following one another with a steady, loping stride, the Indians quickly crossed intervening land to the river or lake which was the next water-link in their journey.

Sources: "From Time To Time…" by Esther Walton, "The Indians and Fur Trading Posts" by Charles Weissert, www.bearfortlodge.com

THE TAVERN: OLDE TOWNE TAVERN CO.

Located in the heart of downtown Hastings at 114 S. Jefferson Street, the building that houses the Olde Towne Tavern Co. has been home to a bar for over 80 years. Since 2005, Rick and Cindy Ester have been the proprietors of the Olde Towne. There's a happy stability in this spot: Rick and Cindy inherited the previous owner's regulars and employees, and the folks on both sides of the bar have stayed the same ever since, with only one change—they now have more stories to tell.

You can see why nobody's leaving this tavern. The help is engaging, pleasant, and leave you with a good feeling about being here. The Olde Towne is a real comfortable watering hole.

Shoot a game of pool on one of the bar's 3 tables, or come in on Fridays or Saturdays for the live music, quite often classic rock.

This is the perfect location to kick back at for something besides the welcoming feel: the Olde Towne Tavern is located a 5 minute walk away from the Thornapple River U-Rent-Em take out point. Reliving the river trip over an Olde Towne Burger, one of "Rick's Wraps", a Perch Dinner, or a few appetizers, tops off your day on the Thornapple very nicely. It's your good fortune that the Olde Towne carries Pabst Blue Ribbons, as a PBR is well-known to be the ideal accompaniment to each of the dishes that the bar serves.

THUNDER BAY RIVER ALPENA, MICHIGAN

RIVER SOUNDTRACK:
Riders On The Storm – the Doors
Recreational Vehicle – Jeff Daniels
I Want To Marry A Lighthouse Keeper
– Erika Eigen
Rainmaker - Traffic
Island – Jimmy Buffett

CANOE LIVERY:
Campers Cove
owners Judy and Mark Hall
5005 Long Rapids Rd. Alpena, Michigan 49707
Phone (989) 356-3708
www.camperscovecampground.com

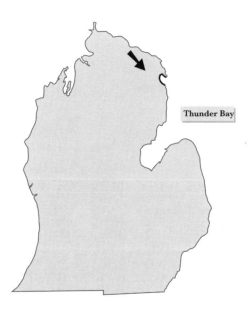

Thunder Bay

Level Two
Intermediate Ability Required

THE BACKGROUND: THUNDER BAY RIVER

Question: how is it possible to add to the enjoyment of a day canoeing down a river? One glorious answer is found on the eastern shoreline, better known as the Sunrise Coast, of the great state of Michigan. The drive along US23 to get to and to depart from Alpena, hugging the Lake Huron shore with its often spectacular views, is a sweet bonus to your day floating down the Thunder Bay River. Sunrise Coast eats are mighty fine, too, starting with one excellent omelet in Omer at Ma's Girls and later in the day for top-rated (by my Dad and my banker, among many others) burgers in Harrisville at Ki Cuyler's Sports Bar & Grill. Ki, also known as Ki-Ki, was born in Harrisville in 1899, & enjoyed an 18-year ('21 to '38) Hall of Fame baseball career (.321 lifetime) with the Pirates and the Cubs. Although Ki passed away during 1950 in Ann Arbor, apparently he had a desire to return home: the pub was built upon the land where his childhood house had once stood, and it is rumored that Ki-Ki gently haunts the bar. Maybe it's hard to find burgers that taste that good where he now resides. Reportedly, a man in a baseball uniform has appeared and just as quickly disappeared, cooked food has materialized, and the dishes cleaned and put away. If it wasn't for the unexplained misplaced pitchers of beer, this would be the perfect ghost.

Thunder Bay River is a pleasant float, with its most enjoyable (and challenging) stretch the "Speechley" or "Long" Rapids, which begin approximately 45 minutes into the ride, and run for an estimated 1,200 feet. Our trip was during the relatively high water time of a rainy early-June. When the water is at its post-June level, these rocky Long Rapids might force you to walk your boat through. Because of this, it is suggested that you canoe the Thunder Bay River early in the season, or after a heavy rain raises the water level.

The Thunder Bay River Exploration Team was Andy Kocembo, Paula Brown, Bobby Kocembo, Kenny Umphrey, Maggie and me.

THE RIVER: PADDLING THUNDER BAY

Suggested trip is a 2 hour and 40 minute float, putting in at Long Rapids Township Park and the M65 Bridge access, just south of Long Rapids Road. There are only two bridges that you will see on this trip: the M65 Bridge where you put in and the Herron Road Bridge where the ride ends. There are no established campgrounds or toilets on this stretch, and during our high water early-season adventure, very few good places where you can pull over for a break. As the trip begins, the river is 70' wide and 2' deep.

7 min. in / 2 hr. 33 min. to go: A tangle of branches extends into the river from the left shore, clogging two-thirds of the river. There is plenty of space to paddle around this along the right shore. As soon as you clear this, cut back left as immediately downstream is additional debris from the right shore.

9 min. in / 2 hrs 31 min. to go: A dead creek merges from the right, adding volume to the river as it deepens to 4'.

19 min. in / 2 hrs 21 min. to go: 40' long island sits on the right side of the river. While the main body of the rivers flows left, you may also pass the island on the right where the river is 4 canoe widths wide, per the crack research team.

30 min. in / 2 hrs 10 min. to go: A firmly entrenched white captain's, or fishing, chair sits on the left bank. A 100' run of light rapids follows.

40 min. in / 2 hrs to go: Screened in gazebo and deck are on the right shore.

43 min. in / 1 hr. 57 min. to go: As the river bends right, a 5 minute long rocky rapids run begins, known to the folks who live in the area as the Speechley, or Long, Rapids. The river depth as the rapids begin is between 6" to 12". This run is an estimated 1,200' long. Even in early-season high water there is a great deal of bottom-skimming, along with actual bottoming out along the left

bank. During these rapids there are two ledges that you paddle over where the river floor drops 4" to 6". There's a great deal of rocks (and fun!) encountered. In the midst of all of this action, a deer races across the river right in front of us, bounding from the left shore to the right.

54 min. in / 1 hr. 46 min. to go: At the end of a long straightaway of calm water, an island lies on the left side of the river, offering side exploration opportunities. As the river bends right, you see rapids activity beginning again, although not as choppy as the Speechly (Long) run.

57 min. in / 1 hr. 43 min. to go: The rapids end as the river bends right. An island sits mid- stream with birch trees along the right shore. A large rock, left of center, is visible 1' above the water line. 2 more mid-river islands lie just downstream. Many beautiful, unobtrusive homes are viewed along the float. Bald eagles accompany us on and off.

1 hr. 10 min. in / 1 hr. 30 min. to go: At the end of a long straightaway, where a home with a deck on stilts sits on the left shore, is a very wide island covering 80% of the river. The island is passable, with bottom-skimming, on both the right and the left. Just beyond the island lies poop rock (christen as such by Dr. Bobbers), an apparently favorite target of the bald eagles and other local birds.

1 hr. 15 min. in / 1 hr. 25 min. to go: As the river bends right, an island is along the river's right. Beautiful fields of fern soon begin to appear, joining us for most of the trip's balance. The river depth is at 2'.
Although there are no rapids, the current is swift.

Kenny Sez: "I have a photographic memory. It's just short"

1 hr. 32 min. in / 1 hr. 8 min. to go: From the top of a long straightaway, it looks as if a gigantic snake inhabits the hillside at the straightaway's end. As earlier some small snakes floated alongside our canoes, there is some distant concern that they may have been scouts for Anacondas (they do average 23' long). Fortunately, this turns out to be a serpentine-shaped seawall. Whew. As active imaginations recede, the river deepens to 4'.

2 hrs in / 40 min. to go: Asparagus appears on the left shore. The river is now 80' across and alternates from 4' deep to 6' deep.

2 hrs 10 min. in / 30 min. to go: Let the driftwood slightly left of the river's center serve as a warning: 10' to the left of the driftwood piece a large rock sits just beneath the water line. This is big and you want to avoid coming in contact with it.

2 hrs 30 min. in / 10 min. to go: A 150 yard rapids run begins. Beware the large rock left of center at the beginning of this rapids.

2 hrs 34 min. in / 6 min. to go: A 120' rapids run is short but intense with standing waves large enough to come into your canoe. On the

next bend is a very large island. Around this island, the main body of the river flows left (60' wide), but there is plenty of room to pass on the right (40' wide), too. There is a small island just downstream.

2 hours and 40 minutes in and the trip is at an end. Paddle under the Herron Bridge and take out just beyond the bridge and on the right.

THE TOWN: ALPENA

Detroit Tigers local radio affiliate: WIDG 940AM (Cheboygan).

Alpena is located near the center of the 200-mile long US23 stretch known as the Sunrise Side Coastal Highway. The town is surrounded by water with Lake Huron to its east and north and Thunder Bay to its south. Alpena's geography makes it a major recreation area, as besides being adjacent to Lake Huron and Thunder Bay, nearby is found Black Lake, Hubbard Lake, Fletcher's Pond (a pond in name only), Long Lake, Grand Lake, and many smaller lakes. Alpena is also a major exporter of limestone and cement, but almost 100 years ago the town was also well known across the Midwest for something totally unrelated to water recreation, or limestone, or cement. From 1910 to 1914, the Alpena Motor Car Company built a car that enjoyed a popular following from as far away as New York to the east and Minnesota to the west: the Alpena Flyer. The Flyer was built for speed, and its loyal customers loved it! The car's appeal never faded, but the Alpena Motor Car Co. was forced into bankruptcy in 1913 when it lost a patent lawsuit.

One of Alpena's most popular tourist attractions is their Great Lakes Maritime Heritage Center. A visit to the Center can include a snorkeling tour among the Lake Huron and Thunder Bay shipwrecks, and a visit to the 7 lighthouses in the area with an opportunity to spend the night on an island and experience the life of a lighthouse keeper.

20 minutes to the north of Alpena is the Old Presque Isle Lighthouse. Presque Isle, pronounced Presk Eel, is French for "almost an island". Built in 1840, this is one of the oldest surviving lighthouses on the Great Lakes. Today, it is a non-working lighthouse, and serves as a museum. One of the many interesting historical items regarding this lighthouse concerns Jefferson Davis. Before his days as president of the Confederacy, Davis had fur trapping interests in the area. He used his influence with Congress to lobby for funds so that the Presque Isle Lighthouse may be built. Another fun historical tidbit is that the doors in the lighthouse keeper's house are built from planks from shipwrecks (and they majestically look it). Finally, a ghost seems to be a regular visitor to the lighthouse. Although the machinery needed to work the lighthouse light was removed, checked and rechecked by the Coast Guard, the light will occasionally shine.

"Lefty's Lament" is a poem written in 1936 by Don S. Olds. It is made available in the lighthouse to all visitors. The poem captures well the feelings held by those who love the north and the sad times when they miss an opportunity to join their friends there. In my mind, I'll take the liberty of substituting "canoe and cooler" for "dog and gun".

Lefty's Lament

It's hell to sit on the sidelines, when the trek to the North has begun,
And wave your friends off with a smile, with their duffel, their dog and their gun.
In our thoughts, we follow them Northward past Tawas and on to Presque Isle,
Till the tang of the pine and the hemlock in our nostrils almost seem real.
We vision the Tower and the Cottage, o'er the harbor appearing in view,

Then the Cabin, dark and deserted, the old giving way to the new.
We tread the cement and the asphalt, not the needles there under the pines;
Hear the screech of tires on pavement, not the wind thru the trees as it whines.
And the thought that carries us onward is the hope that we soon may be there.
With the play and the work and the laughter, that now we are longing to share.

Sources: www.rootsweb.com, "Michigan Yesterday and Today" by Ferris Lewis, www.alpenacvb.com, Poems by Don S. Olds

THE TAVERN: THE OLDE OWL TAVERN & GRILLE

As Ki Cuyler's Sports Bar & Grill is 32 miles away, you may wish to opt for a tavern a bit closer to the river. In downtown Alpena, an enjoyable and relaxing post-canoeing time may be had at the Olde Owl Tavern & Grille. The Olde Owl, located along US23, is more of a restaurant than a pub, although the Owl has a bar that welcomes you to belly up to it.

Our group was very pleased with the food, and we left fat and happy. I would be remiss if I did not mention that the Olde Owl stocks Pabst Blue Ribbon longnecks, a sure sign of quality.

PADDLING/CAMPING CHECK LIST

TIPS TO MAKE YOUR ADVENTURE A LITTLE EASIER

- ☐ Bug spray/mosquito hat
- ☐ Plastic drop cloths (in case of rain)
- ☐ Dry bags (waterproof)
- ☐ Water
- ☐ Forks, plates, pots, pans, large spoon
- ☐ Aluminum foil or food wrap (leftovers)
- ☐ Lange and small Ziplock bags
- ☐ Hat or baseball cap
- ☐ Hand towel/ paper plates
- ☐ Suntan lotion/sun block
- ☐ Trash bags
- ☐ First aid kit
- ☐ Food
- ☐ Portable music/batteries
- ☐ Nose strips (for your loud friends)
- ☐ Ear plugs (see nose strips)
- ☐ Small pillow
- ☐ Irwin saw
- ☐ Clothes line rope
- ☐ Blankets
- ☐ Flashlights
- ☐ Rain poncho
- ☐ Dry box (waterproof)

- ☐ Soap, toothbrush toothpaste
- ☐ Euchre decks
- ☐ Camera/film or digital camera
- ☐ River chairs
- ☐ Money and wallet
- ☐ Sunglasses
- ☐ Sleeping bag
- ☐ Knife
- ☐ Firestarter, matches
- ☐ Two sets of car keys
- ☐ Thermarest/ air-mattress
- ☐ Bungee cords
- ☐ Frisbees
- ☐ Towels
- ☐ Toilet paper
- ☐ Cooler, ice, water
- ☐ River clothes/dry clothes
- ☐ River shoes/dry shoes
- ☐ Grill/grate
- ☐ Tent
- ☐ Aspirin
- ☐ Bug spray - with DEET
- ☐ Can opener/bottle opener

MICHIGAN CANOE LIVERIES UPPER PENINSULA RIVERS

AU TRAIN RIVER

Northwoods Resort 906-892-8114
N7070 AuTrain Forest Lake Rd, AuTrain, MI 49806
www.northwoodsresort.net

BRULE RIVER

Michi-Aho Resort 906-875-3514
2181 M-69, Crystal Falls, MI 49920
www.michiahoresort.com

NORTHWOODS WILDERNESS OUTFITTERS 906-774-9009, 1-800-530-8859
N-4088 Pine Mountain Road, Iron Mountain, MI 49801
www.northwoodsoutfitters.com

CARP RIVER

U. P. Wide Adventure Guide 906-430-0547
W6508 Epoufette Bay Road, Naubinway, MI 49762
www.upwideadventureguide.com

ESCANABA RIVER

Uncle Ducky Outfitters 906-228-5447, 877-228-5447
434 E. Prospect, Marquette, MI 49855
www.uncleduckyoutfitters.com

FORD RIVER

Mr. Rental 906-789-7776, 877-906-7776
627 Stephenson Ave., Escanaba, MI 49829

FOX RIVER

Big Cedar Campground & Canoe Livery 906-586-6684
7936 State Hwy. M-77, Germfask, MI 49836
www.bigcedarcampground.com

Northland Outfitters 906-586-9801, 800-808-3FUN
8174 Hwy M-77, Germfask, MI 49836
www.northoutfitters.com

MANISTIQUE RIVER

Big Cedar Campground & Canoe Livery 906-586-6684
7936 State Hwy. M-77, Germfask, MI 49836
www.bigcedarcampground.com

Northland Outfitters 906-586-9801, 800-808-3FUN
8174 Hwy M-77, Germfask, MI 49836
www.northoutfitters.com

U. P. Wide Adventure Guide 906-430-0547
W6508 Epoufette Bay Road, Naubinway, MI 49762
www.upwideadventureguide.com

MENOMINEE RIVER

Northwoods Wilderness Outfitters 906-774-9009, 1-800-530-8859
N-4088 Pine Mountain Road, Iron Mountain, MI 49801
www.northwoodsoutfitters.com

MICHIGAMME RIVER

Michi-Aho Resort 906-875-3514
2181 M-69, Crystal Falls, MI 49920
www.michiahoresort.com

Northwoods Wilderness Outfitters 906-774-9009, 1-800-530-8859
N-4088 Pine Mountain Road, Iron Mountain, MI 49801
www.northwoodsoutfitters.com

Uncle Ducky Outfitters 906-228-5447, 877-228-5447
434 E. Prospect, Marquette, MI 49855
www.uncleduckyoutfitters.com

MILLECOQUINS RIVER

U. P. Wide Adventure Guide 906-430-0547
W6508 Epoufette Bay Road, Naubinway, MI 49762
www.upwideadventureguide.com

ONTONAGON RIVER

Sylvania Outfitters, Inc. 906-358-4766
E23423 Hwy. 2, Watersmeet, MI 49969
www.sylvaniaoutfitters.com

PAINT RIVER

Michi-Aho Resort 906-875-3514
2181 M-69, Crystal Falls, MI 49920
www.michiahoresort.com

Northwoods Wilderness Outfitters 906-774-9009, 1-800-530-8859
N-4088 Pine Mountain Road, Iron Mountain, MI 49801
www.northwoodsoutfitters.com

PINE RIVER

U. P. Wide Adventure Guide 906-430-0547
W6508 Epoufette Bay Road, Naubinway, MI 49762
www.upwideadventureguide.com

TAHQUAMEMON RIVER

Tahquamenon General Store Canoe & Kayak Rentals 906-429-3560
39991 W. Highway 123, Paradise, MI 49768

The Woods 906-203-7624
P.O. Box 536, Newberry, MI 49868

U. P. Wide Adventure Guide 906-430-0547
W6508 Epoufette Bay Road, Naubinway, MI 49762
www.upwideadventureguide.com

TWO HEARTED RIVER

Two Hearted Canoe Trips, Inc., 906- 658-3357
32752 County Road 423, Newberry, MI 49868
www.rainbowlodgemi.com

U. P. Wide Adventure Guide 906-430-0547
W6508 Epoufette Bay Road, Naubinway, MI 49762
www.upwideadventureguide.com

LOWER PENINSULA RIVERS

AU SABLE RIVER

Alcona Canoe Rental & Campground   989-735-2973, 800-526-7080
6351 Bamfield Road, Glennie, MI 48737
www.alconacanoes.com

Bear Paw Cabins & Canoe Livery 989-826-3313
3744 W. M72, Luzerne, MI 48636

Borcher's Ausable Canoe Livery 989-348-4921, 800-762-8756
101 Maple St., Grayling, MI 49738
www.canoeborchers.com

Carlisle Canoes 989-348-2301
110 State St, Grayling, MI 49738
www.carlislecanoes.com

Enchanted Acres Campground 231-266-5102
9581 N. Brooks Rd., Irons, MI 49644
www.enchantedacrescamp.com

Gott's Landing 989-826-3411, 888-226-8748 (Reservations only)
701 N. Morenci Rd., Mio, MI 48647
www.gottslanding.com

Hinchman Acres 989-826-3267, 800-438-0203
702 N. M-33, P. O. Box 220, Mio, MI 48647
www.hinchman.com

Jim's Canoe (989) 348-3203
1706 Wakeley Bridge Rd., Grayling, MI 49738
www.jimscanoe.com

Oscoda Canoe Rental 989-739-9040
678 River Rd., Oscoda, MI 48750
www.oscodacanoe.com

Penrod's AuSable River Resort 888-467-4837, 989-348-2910
100 Maple St., Grayling, MI 49738
www.penrodscanoe.com

Rollway Resort 989-728-3322
6160 Rollways Road, Hale, MI 48739
www.rollwayresort.com

Watters Edge Canoe Livery 989-275-5568, 800-672-9968
10799 Dana Dr., Roscommon, MI 48653
www.wecl.8k.com

AUSABLE, SOUTH BRANCH

Canoe At Campbell's 989-275-5810, 800-722-6633
1112 Lake St., Roscommon, MI 48653
www.canoeatcampbells.com

Hiawatha Canoe Livery 888-515-5213, 989-275-5213
1113 Lake Street, Roscommon, MI 48653
www.canoehiawatha.com

Jim's Canoe (989) 348-3203
1706 Wakeley Bridge Rd., Grayling, MI 49738
www.jimscanoe.com

Paddle Brave Canoe Livery & Campground 989-275-5273, 800-681-7092
10610 Steckert Bridge Rd., Roscommon, MI 48653
www.paddlebrave.com

Parmalee Trading Post 989-826-3543
78 N. Red Oak Rd, Lewiston, MI 49756

Watters Edge Canoe Livery 989-275-5568, 800-672-9968
10799 Dana Dr., Roscommon, MI 48653
www.wecl.8k.com

BEAR RIVER

Bear River Canoe Livery 231-347-9038, 231-838-4141
2517 McDougal, Petosky, MI 49770

BETSIE RIVER

Alvina's Canoe and Boat Rental 231-276-9514
6470 Betsie River Rd. S, Interlochen, MI 49643

Betsie River Canoes & Campground 231- 879-3850
13598 Lindy Rd./Highway 602, Thompsonville, MI 49683
www.betsierivercanoseandcampground.com

Hanmer's Riverside Resort 231-882-7783
2251 Benzie Hwy, Benzonia, MI 49616
www.hammers.com

Vacation Trailer Park Inc. 231-882-5101
2080 Benzie Hwy., Benzonia, MI 49616
www.vacationtrailer.com

BOARDMAN RIVER

Boardman Paddle & Peddle 231-944-1146
205 Garland St., Traverse City, MI 49684
www.boardmanpaddleandpeddle.com

Ranch Rudolf 231-947-9529
6841 Brown Bridge Rd., Traverse City, MI 49686
www.ranchrudolf.com

BLACK RIVER (Northern Lower Peninsula)

Black River Canoe Outfitters/Ma & Pa's Country Store 989-733-8054
M33 & Hackett Lake Rd., Onaway, MI 49765

CASS RIVER

Cork pine Canoe Rental 989-863-0103
132 S. Water St., Vassar, MI 48768
www.corkpinecanoerental.com

CHIPPEWA RIVER

Buckley's Mountainside Canoes 989-772-5437, 877-776-2800
4700 W. Remus Rd., Mt. Pleasant, MI 48858
www.buckleyscanoes.com

Chippewa River Outfitters 989-772-5474, 888-775-6077
3763 S. Lincoln Rd., Mt Pleasant, MI 48858
www.chipoutfitters.com

COLDWATER RIVER

Indian Valley 616-891-8579,
8200 108th, Middleville, MI 49333
www.indianvalleycampgroundandcanoe.com

CRYSTAL RIVER

Crystal River Outfitters 231-334-4420
6249 W. River Rd., Glen Arbor, MI 49696
www.crystalriveroutfitters.com

DOWAGIAC RIVER

Doe-Wah-Jack's Canoe Rental Inc. 888-782-7410, 269-782-7410
52963 M-51 N., Dowagiac, MI 49047
www.paddledcri.com

FAWN RIVER

Liquid Therapy Canoe & Kayak Rentals 269-273-9000
221 S. Main St., Three Rivers, MI 49093
www.liquidtherapypaddling.com

FLAT RIVER

Double R Ranch Resort 616-794-0520
4424 Whites Bridge Rd., Belding, MI 48809
www.doublerranch.com

GRAND RIVER

Grand Adventures 517-712-6475, 517-628-3046
4590 Onondaga Rd., Onondaga, MI 49264

Grand Rogue Campground and Canoe 616-361-1053
6400 West River Dr., Belmont, MI 49306
www.grandrogue.com

HERSEY RIVER

Hersey Canoe Livery 231-832-7220
625 E. 4th St., Hersey, MI 49639
www.herseycanoe.com

HURON RIVER

Ann Arbor Canoe Livery (Gallup Park)734-662-9319
3000 Fuller Rd., Ann Arbor, MI 48105

Argo Canoe Livery 734-668-7411
1055 Longshore Dr., Ann Arbor, MI 48109

Heavner Canoe Rental 248-685-2379
2775 Garden Rd., Milford, MI 48381
www.heavnercanoe.com

Skip's Huron River Canoe Livery 734-768-8686
3780 Delhi Ct., Ann Arbor, MI 48103

Village Canoe Rental 248-685-9207
1216 Garden, Milford, MI 48381
www.villagecanoerental.com

JORDAN RIVER

Jordan Valley Outfitters 231-536-0006
311 N. Lake St. (M-66), East Jordan, MI 49727
www.jvoutfitters.com

Swiss Hideaway, Inc 231-536-2341
1953 Graves Crossing, Mancelona, MI 49659
www.jordanriverfun.com

KALAMAZOO RIVER

Old Allegan Canoe /Kayaker's Run 269-561-5481
2722 Old Allegan Rd, Fennville, MI 49408
www.oldallegancanoe.com

Twin Pines Campground and Canoe Livery 517-524-6298
9800 Wheeler Rd., Hanover, MI 49241

LOOKING GLASS RIVER

Wacousta Canoe Livery 517-626-6873
9988 Riverside Drive, Eagle, MI 48822

LITTLE MANISTEE RIVER

Enchanted Acres Campground 231-266-5102
9581 N. Brooks Rd., Irons, MI 49644
www.enchantedacrescamp.com

Pine Creek Lodge 231-848-4431
13544 Caberfae Hwy., Wellston, MI 49689
www.pinecreeklodge.net

LITTLE MUSKEGON RIVER

Bob & Pat's White Birch Canoe Trips & Campground 231-328-4547
Paradise Rd., Falmouth, MI 49632
www.whitebirchcanoe.com

Wisner Rents Canoes 231-652-6743
25 W. Water St., Newaygo, MI 49337
www.wisnercanoes.com

MANISTEE RIVER

Chippewa Landing 231-313-0832
10420 Chippewa Landing Trail, Manton, MI 49663
www.chippewalanding.com

Enchanted Acres Campground 231-266-5102
9581 N. Brooks Rd., Irons, MI 49644
www.enchantedacrescamp.com

Long's Canoe Livery 989-348-7224, 231-258-3452
8341 M-72 N.E., Kalkaska, MI 49646
www.longscanoelivery.com

Missaukee Paddle Sports 231-839-8265
214 S. Main Street, Lake City, MI 49651
www.missaukeepaddlesports.com

Pine Creek Lodge 231-848-4431
13544 Caberfae Hwy., Wellston, MI 49689
www.pinecreeklodge.net

Pine River Paddlesports Center 231-862-3471,
9590 Grand View Hwy. S37, Wellston, MI 49689
www.thepineriver.com

Shel-Haven Canoe Rental 989-348-2158
P.O.Box 268, Grayling,MI 49738
www.shelhaven.com

Smithville Landing 231-839-4579
M-66 on the Manistee River P.O.Box 341, Lake City, MI 49651
www.smithvillelanding.com

Wilderness Canoe Trips 800-873-6379, 231-885-1485
6052 Riverview Rd., Mesick, MI 49668
www.wildernesscanoetripsonline.com

MAPLE RIVER

Maple River Campground 989-981-6792
15420 French Rd., Pewamo, MI 48873

MUSKEGON RIVER

Bob & Pat's White Birch Canoe Trips & Campground 231-328-4547
Paradise Rd., Falmouth, MI 49632
www.whitebirchcanoe.com

Duggan's Canoe Livery 989-539-7149
3100 N. Temple Drive, Harrison, MI 48625

Hersey Canoe Livery 231-832-7220
625 E. 4th St., Hersey, MI 49639
www.herseycanoe.com

Missaukee Paddle Sports 231-839-8265
214 S. Main Street, Lake City, MI 49651
www.missaukeepaddlesports.com

Muskegon River Camp & Canoe 231-734-3808
River Country Campground (New Name)
6281 River Rd., Evart, MI 49631
www.campandcanoe.com

Old Log Resort 231-743-2775
12062 M-115, Marion, MI 49665
www.oldlogresort.com

River Rat Canoe Rental 231-834-9411
8702 River Dr. Bridgeton Twnshp, Grant, MI 49327
www.riverratcanoerental.com

Salmon Run Campground & Vic's Canoes 231-834-5495
8845 Felch Ave., Grant, MI 49327
www.salmonrunmi.com

Sawmill Tube and Canoe Livery 231-796-6408
230 Baldwin St., Big Rapids, MI 49307
www.sawmillmi.com

Wisner Rents Canoes 231-652-6743
25 W. Water St., Newaygo, MI 49337
www.wisnercanoes.com

PERE MARQUETTE RIVER

    Baldwin Canoe Rental 231-745-4669, 800-272-3642
    9117 South M37, P. O. Box 269, Baldwin, MI 49304
    www.baldwincanoe.com

    Ivan's Canoe Rental 231-745-3361, 231-745-9345
    7332 South M-37, Baldwin, MI 49304
    www.ivanscanoe.com

    River Run Canoe Livery 231-757-2266
    600 S Main St., Scottville, MI 49454
    www.riverruncanoerental.com

PIGEON RIVER (NORTHERN-LOWER PENINSULA)

    Big Bear Adventures 231-238-8181
    4271 S. Straits Hwy., Indian River, MI 49749
    www.bigbearadventures.com

PIGEON RIVER (SOUTHERN-LOWER PENINSULA)

    Liquid Therapy Canoe & Kayak Rentals 269-273-9000
    221 S. Main St., Three Rivers, MI 49093
    www.liquidtherapypaddling.com

PINEBOG RIVER

    Tip-O-Thumb Canoe & Kayak Rental 989-738-7656
    2475 Port Austin Rd., Port Austin, MI 48467

PINE RIVER

    Enchanted Acres Campground 231-266-5102
    9581 N. Brooks Rd., Irons, MI 49644
    www.enchantedacrescamp.com

    Horina Canoe & Kayak Rental 231-862-3470
    9889 M-37 South, Wellston, Michigan 49689
    www.horinacanoe.com

    Pine River Paddlesports Center 231-862-3471,
    9590 Grand View Hwy. S37, Wellston, MI 49689
    www.thepineriver.com

Shlomer Canoes & Kayaks 231-862-3475
11390 N. M-37, Irons, MI 49644
www.shomlercanoes.com

Sportsman's Port Canoes, Campground 231- 862-3571, 888-226-6301
4020 E. 46 Mile Rd., Cadillac, MI 49601
www.sportsmansport.com

Wilderness Canoe Trips 800-873-6379, 231-885-1485
6052 Riverview Rd., Mesick, MI 49668
www.wildernesscanoetripsonline.com

PLATTE RIVER

Riverside Canoes 231-325-5622
5042 Scenic Hwy., Honor, MI 49640
www.canoemichigan.com

PORTAGE RIVER, PRAIRIE RIVER, ROCKY RIVER

Liquid Therapy Canoe & Kayak Rentals 269-273-9000
221 S. Main St., Three Rivers, MI 49093
www.liquidtherapypaddling.com

RED CEDAR RIVER

MSU Bikes 517-432-3400
B10 Bessey Hall, East Lansing, MI 48824
www.bikes.msu.edu/canoe-rentals.html

RIFLE RIVER

Big Mike's Canoe Rental 989-473-3444
2575 Rose City Rd., Lupton, MI 48635
www.canoe4rent.com

Cedar Springs Campground, Canoe 989-654-3195,
334 Melita Rd., Sterling, MI 48659

River View Campground & Canoe Livery 989-654-2447
5755 N. Town Line Rd., Sterling, MI 48659
www.riverviewcampground.com

Russell Canoes & Campgrounds 989-653-2644
146 Carrington St., Omer, MI 48749
www.russellcanoe.com

Troll Landing Campground & Canoe Livery 989-345-7260
2660 Rifle River Trail, West Branch, MI 48661
www.trolllanding.com

White's Canoe Livery 989-654-2654
400 Old M-70, Sterling, MI 48659
www.whitescanoe.com

RIVER RAISIN

River Raisin Canoe Livery 734-529-9029
1151 Plank Rd., Dundee, MI 48131
www.riverraisincanoelivery.com

ROGUE RIVER

AAA Canoe Rental 616-866-9264
525 Northland Dr., Rockford, MI 49341
www.aaacanoerental.com

Powers Outdoors 616-863-8107
65 Main St., Rockford, Mi 49341
www.powersoutdoors.com

ROUGE RIVER

Heavner Canoe Rental 248-685-2379
2775 Garden Rd., Milford, MI 48381
www.heavnercanoe.com

SHIAWASSEE RIVER

Walnut Hills Campgrounds, Canoe 989-634-9782
7685 Lehring Rd., Durand, MI 48429
www.walnuthillsresort.com

St. Joseph River

Liquid Therapy Canoe & Kayak Rentals 269-273-9000
221 S. Main St., Three Rivers, MI 49093
www.liquidtherapypaddling.com

Sturgeon River

Big Bear Adventures 231-238-8181
4271 S. Straits Hwy., Indian River, MI 49749
www.bigbearadventures.com

Henley's Canoe & Kayak Rental 213-525-9994
13062 Rail Road St., Wolverine, MI 49799
www.henleysrentals.com

Thornapple River

Indian Valley 616-891-8579,
8200 108th, Middleville, MI 49333
www.indianvalleycampgroundandcanoe.com

U-Rent-Em Canoe Livery (269) 945-3191
805 W Apple St., Hastings, Michigan 49058
urentemcanoe.com

Whispering Waters Campground and Canoes 269-945-5166
1805 N. Irving Rd., Hastings, MI 49058
www.whisperingwatersonline.com

Thunder Bay River

Campers Cove Campground and Canoe 888-306-3708, 989-356-3708
5005 Long Rapids Rd., Alpena, MI 49707
www.camperscovecampground.com

Thunder Bay River Canoe & Kayak 989-785-2187
12520 Airport Rd., Atlanta, MI 49709
www.thunderbaycanoeing.com

WHITE RIVER

Happy Mohawk Canoe Livery 231-894-4209
735 Fruitvale Rd., Montague, MI 49437
www.happymohawk.com

Kellogg's Canoes 231-854-1415
P.O. Box 272, Hesperia, MI 49421

Powers Outdoors 231-893-8107, 616-863-8107
4523 Dowling St., Mi 49437
www.powersadventures.com

THE END OF THE TRAIL

ABOUT THE AUTHOR

Doc Fletcher was born Jeffrey Marc Fletcher in Detroit, Michigan, in 1954. He moved with his family to Lambertville, Michigan, in 1967. Doc graduated from Bedford High School (Go Mules!) in 1972 and from Eastern Michigan University (Once a Huron, Always a Huron!) in 1976.

Doc married his favorite Huron, Maggie Meeker, on the shores of the Huron River in 1981. They live together in Northville.

After 30 rewarding years working for Duracell, Doc retired in 2006 to work full time on paddling rivers and writing about the experiences.

Weekend Canoeing In Michigan, released in 2007, was Doc's previous book.